Break Through

The Merrill Linguistic Reading Program
Third Edition
Based on the philosophy
of Charles C. Fries

Authors:
Rosemary G. Wilson
Mildred K. Rudolph

Consultants:
Heather Elko
Timothy E. Heron
Lois Michel Plous
Betsy Small
Goldie Wilson

Editorial Coordinator:
Judith Willard Kinney

Production Coordinator:
Gwendolyn Joslin Hiles

Editor:
Ruth Bradfield Cochrane

Contributing Editors:
Deborah C. Damian
Barbara A. Everett
Jeannetta Perkins Holliman

Project Designer:
Richard C. Cantrell

Project Artist:
R. Ann Diehl

Charles E. Merrill Publishing Co.
A Bell & Howell Company
London·Toronto·Sydney

TABLE OF CONTENTS

Moving In	6
Emergency Numbers	10
Grandma and the Twins	12
In the White House	17
Sick or Well?	22
Care of a Turtle	25
A Winter Day	28
The Girl Who Wouldn't Give Up	33
The First Plane Ride	40
A Basketball for Dan	46
The Peach-Basket Game	51
Fishing for Fun	56
The Job of Catching Fish	58
A Good Catch	60
A Team	64
A Fine Helper	65
On the Yellow Plains of Africa	70
Dr. Jenson's Tall Problem	73
Music in the Home	78
The First Music	81
A Night To Remember	84
A City Map	88

Published by
Charles E. Merrill Publishing Co.
A Bell & Howell Company
Columbus, Ohio 43216

Copyright © 1980, 1975, 1966 by Bell & Howell Company
All rights reserved. No part of this book may be reproduced in any form, electronic or mechanical, including photocopy, recording, or any information storage or retrieval system, without permission in writing from the publisher.
Printed in the United States of America   **ISBN-0-675-01164-7**

My Teacher and I	90
Life on a Ranch	92
Dinner for All	98
Let's Make a Salad	103
The Toy Sale	106
Falling Snow	111
The Lesson	114
In the News Today	118
The Golden Touch	120
Mr. Nobody	127
A Girl in Space	130
Helping Hands	136
Mountain Lions	140
Good Ideas	142
The Secret	146
Reading a Work Schedule	151

To the Teacher	152

live
give
forgive
olive

lift　　　gave　　　give　　　olive
live　　　give　　　live　　　forgive
olive　　forgive　　river

Moving In

One of the houses on Grove Street was empty. The Bentons, who had lived there, were on their way to a new home. All the neighbors were sad to see them leave.

Traffic was bad on the way to the new house in Riverside. But in much less than an hour Mrs. Benton stopped the car in front of their new house. The family got out and stood looking at their new home. Mr. Benton smiled and said, "I think we'll be very happy here."

Just then the moving van drove up. The movers began to bring tables, beds, and chests into the house. They kept asking which things went into which rooms. At last they finished unloading the van. They set up the beds. Then they left for their next job.

The Bentons had a lot of work to do in getting settled. Mr. Benton dusted and ran the sweeper. Mrs. Benton cleaned the kitchen. Her mother, Mrs.

Lang, unpacked sheets and blankets. First she went into Jim's room and fixed the bottom bunk bed. "I'll leave the top one for now," she said to herself. Mr. Benton fixed the bed in Kim's room. Then Mrs. Lang fixed up the front bedroom and the spare room.

Jim and Kim were not upstairs with Grandma. And they were not in the kitchen. Mrs. Lang called, "Sally, have you seen Jim and Kim?"

"They're in the basement," said Mrs. Benton. "They had boxes to unpack. I'm sure they'll come up here when they get hungry."

"Well, I packed lunches for all of us last night," said Grandma. "I used all those odds and ends you didn't want to waste. I have roast beef sandwiches, meat loaf sandwiches, and a salad with lots of olives."

Grandma had apples, peaches, and a big pitcher of iced tea, too. As she was filling the five glasses, Kim crept into the room. Grandma finished filling the last glass. She turned to set the pitcher back on the counter.

"Oh, Kim!" she gasped. "You did give me a scare! I nearly dropped this iced tea!"

"Forgive me, Grandma," said Kim. "I wanted to give you a surprise, but it wasn't a very nice surprise, was it? Please forgive me."

"Oh, I forgive you, Kim," said Grandma. "I forgive you, but don't do it any more."

Then Grandma added, "As long as you're here, you can have your lunch. Scrub your hands, and I'll call Jim."

Kim turned on the water in the sink and held her hands under it. She began to shiver and said, "This feels like ice water. I think I'll wait till it gets hot."

"That will be a while," said Mrs. Benton. "The water heater isn't connected yet."

Jim came into the kitchen. He and Kim managed to get clean without hot water. They had just finished lunch when Mr. Benton came into the kitchen. "I hope you left something for me. I'm really hungry!" he said. He went to the sink to

8

wash his hands. But when he looked at it, he said, "What a mess! The people who lived here might have left us a cleaner sink!"

"They did leave a clean sink, Mark," said Mrs. Lang. "Jim and Kim are the ones who did that."

"I might as well clean it while I'm here," said Mr. Benton.

A week later Grandma Lang was still helping the Bentons get settled. One day Mrs. Benton said, "It's good to have you here, Mother. Mark and I wish you would come to live with us. We have plenty of room in this big house. Please say yes!"

"I'd like to, Sally," said Grandma. "But I can't be sure. Give me a little time to think it over."

Emergency Numbers

When you are making emergency calls, speak clearly. Tell the person what you want. Give the exact address where help is needed. Do not hang up the phone until the other person has hung up.

Use the first page of the telephone book to tell which number to call in your town for each of the following.

1. What number would you call to report a fire?
2. If you needed an ambulance, what number would you call?
3. If you needed the police, what number would you call?
4. Is the number for the fire department and for the ambulance the same?
5. Is there a number listed for the county sheriff?
6. What other emergency numbers are listed?
7. In any emergency, if you don't know what number to call, who can you always call?

love

glove

shove

cover

done

none

once

warm

give	love	nine	one
live	glove	none	ones
love	shove	done	once

Grandma and the Twins

Grandma Lang stayed with the Bentons for another week. On some days she felt restless and wanted to go back to her apartment. On other days she felt sure she wanted to live with the Bentons all the time. They were all the family she had.

Mrs. Lang had mixed feelings about living with the twins. She didn't care if they were loud sometimes. But when they shoved each other trying to get to the TV first, she would get upset. "One of them might trip and fall," she said to herself. She liked the music they played on the record player, even when it was loud. But she had to cover her ears when she heard them dancing above her.

But in spite of all these things, Mrs. Lang was always glad to see Jim and Kim come home from school. One day Mrs. Benton called from her shop. "I've broken a tooth," she said. "I must see the dentist in the office on North Street at once. I'm not sure when I'll be home."

"That's all right," said Grandma Lang. "Jim, Kim, and I can go to the market and get something good for dinner. I hope the dentist can fix your tooth."

Grandma placed the lunch dishes in the dishwasher. Then she sat down to write a list for the market. "I think I'll make that chicken and rice dish," she said to herself. "It would be good with green beans and a salad."

Soon Jim and Kim came home from school and quickly changed into old jeans. When they came downstairs, they each had a glass of milk. Grandma told them their mother would be late getting home. "We're in charge of dinner," she said. "How about my chicken and rice dish?"

"That sounds good to me," said Jim.

"OK, do you want to go to the market with me?" asked Grandma.

"Sure," said Kim. "You'll need help carrying those big bags home."

Before long they were back home with three sacks of things. "It's a good thing you did go," said Grandma. "One person couldn't have carried all this. You can play or study while I fix dinner. Since it's warm, why don't you go outside?"

"Thanks, Grandma," said Jim. "I love you."

"I love you, too," said Grandma. "I hope everyone loves my chicken and rice."

Once Jim and Kim had left, Grandma mixed her chicken and rice dish. She covered it and shoved it into a hot oven. "That should take about an hour," she said to herself.

Then Mrs. Lang went outside to do her jogging. She always ran for a while every day before dinner. She passed Kim and Jim playing catch. Kim had a pitcher's glove, and Jim had a catcher's glove. "Those baseball gloves look quite worn. I will have to get them new ones for their birthday," Mrs. Lang said to herself as she jogged along.

Mr. Benton came home just as Mrs. Lang returned from her run. "Sally broke a tooth and had to see a dentist," said Grandma, puffing a little. "I'm keeping dinner warm in the oven."

"I'll set the table while you cool off a bit," said Mr. Benton. "I think I'll make one of my good salads tonight."

"Thanks, Mark. I'll get the beans done in a little bit," said Grandma.

Just as everything was done, Jim and Kim ran in. While they were washing their hands, Mrs. Benton came home. At six o'clock on the dot they all sat down for dinner. When Grandma took the cover off the chicken, it smelled so good.

"I love having you with us, Mother," said Mrs. Benton. "I'm sure it's been good for Jim and Kim to have you around, too. I wish you'd come to stay with us."

"Well," said Grandma, "maybe I will come to stay with you sometime later on. But I miss my apartment and my things. I think on Sunday I'll go back to my apartment for a while."

Photo by Lloyd Ostendorf

In the White House
Anne Colver

Many people have left their old homes for new ones. This story is about some of the problems of Willie and Tad Lincoln in their new home, the White House.

It was the year 1861. Abraham Lincoln was President of the United States. The Lincolns were going to live in the White House.

When it was time to leave for Washington, Willie and Tad Lincoln were sad. It was exciting to have their father elected President. But the boys did not want to leave their home in Springfield.

They begged to take their dog with them. Fido belonged partly to Willie and Tad and partly to their best friends, the Roll boys.

"How can we take part of Fido?" asked Abe Lincoln. "We don't know which part is ours!" Then, to cheer the boys, he said they could have a pony in Washington. Fido was left in Springfield.

Adapted from *Abraham Lincoln: For the People*, copyright 1960 by Anne Colver, with permission of Garrard Publishing Co., Champaign, Illinois.

Soon Mr. Lincoln's family found that the President had to work hard all day long. On many days Mr. Lincoln could not leave his office till late at night. But as hard as he was working, he still kept his promise to his sons. He got them a pony.

Even with a pony to play with, the boys were restless. They were lonely for their friends back home. Their mother was lonely, too. Many times they wanted to be back in Springfield, where Mr. Lincoln had more time to be with them.

Then the War Between the States began. The President had to work even harder. He still played with the boys when he could. Or he took Mrs. Lincoln for a drive. But night after night, the lights were on in the President's office. Mr. Lincoln had to talk to the generals of the Northern army. Then he alone had to judge the best thing to do.

"The North thinks that keeping slaves is wrong," Mr. Lincoln said. "The South does not want to be part of the United States. Each side thinks that it is right. Each side has brave men fighting for it."

The President walked back and forth, back and forth in his office each day. He was waiting to be told the number of men killed in battle. Mr. Lincoln felt sad about each one, whether the man had been fighting for the North or for the South.

One day Willie and Tad wanted to see their dad. For a long time they waited restlessly by his office. Then a visitor finished speaking with the President and left. The boys slipped in. They played near their dad's desk for hours. The President went on with his work. He was not disturbed by his sons playing near him.

Later the President held a cabinet meeting in his office. Tad and Willie hid under the table where the important men sat. When the boys went on playing around the men's feet, the men became angry. They felt the boys did not belong in the room, disturbing older people at their work.

Mr. Lincoln said, "We can't help our boys who are fighting and being killed in battle. But we can let these boys have fun while they can. I don't want to shut them out."

Illustration by Lloyd Ostendorf

head
dead
read
ready
bread
thread
instead
already

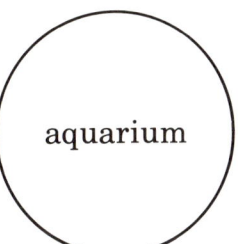

Sick or Well?

It was just past three o'clock on a cold Friday afternoon in November. Mr. Kelly's class was getting ready to go home. They were carrying their coats from their lockers to their desks.

"Hold still, Jen," called Mr. Kelly. "A thread from your scarf is snagged on the aquarium. Abby, please see if you can help her."

Jen stood still as Abby worked to untangle the thread. It was stuck on the metal edge of the aquarium. While Abby worked on the thread, Jen looked into the turtle tank. Then Abby said, "There, Jenny! You're free! I hope your scarf can be fixed."

"Thanks, Abby," said Jen. But instead of looking at her scarf, she went quickly to talk to Mr. Kelly.

"May I ask you something?" she said.

"Yes, certainly," said the teacher.

"If we leave the turtle here all weekend in the cold, will it be dead when we come back on Monday?" Jen asked.

Abby had come along with Jen. She wanted to say something, too. "Mr. Kelly," she said, "I think our turtle is very sick already. I was there in the woods when Manny found it resting on a log in the sun. Its head was out of its shell then. But all this week it's been keeping its head tucked inside its shell."

Mr. Kelly looked at Jen to see if she had anything to add. So far he hadn't spoken at all.

Jen went on, "When Manny tapped the turtle just a little, it started to crawl up the road. This week it has hardly moved at all."

Abby said, "I dropped some bread into the aquarium. The turtle wouldn't even go near it."

"Well," said the teacher, "these things don't prove the turtle is sick. It's too bad Manny isn't in school today. He could answer your questions, I'm sure."

"Please tell us how to take care of the turtle, Mr. Kelly," said Jennifer.

By this time some of the others in the class had come close to listen. Some of them began to tell the girls things that might help.

At last Mr. Kelly spoke. He said, "Instead of telling you how to take care of the turtle, I can think of something even better. Here, I'll give you this book from the library. It's the same one Manny read after he found the turtle."

The teacher went on speaking to the children. He said, "Don't feel sad. I'm sure our turtle will be alive when you come to school on Monday. Just relax and have a good weekend."

Illustration by Holly Zapp

Care of a Turtle
Gertrude Pels

Small turtles make good pets that aren't hard to care for. Turtles can live in a glass aquarium with a pile of large stones in the middle or in a corner. Then the turtles can crawl up out of the water whenever they feel like it. You can stack the stones to make an underwater hiding place, too.

Turtles like to sit in a dry, sunny spot for hours at a time. So keep the tank in a fairly light place. Turtles like to have a sunbath each day. But they cannot stay in the hot sun too long. They should always have a shady place to hide.

If turtles get sick, they should have as much sunshine as possible. But do not "bake" them. Remove them from the sun after an hour or so. Then return them later for more sun.

Turtles eat raw lean beef, raw fish, lettuce, and

From *The Care of Water Pets* by Gertrude Pels.
Copyright 1955 by Gertrude Pels.
With permission of Thomas Y. Crowell Co., Inc.

cooked chicken. Ground-up fish bones will help harden a turtle's shell. Turtles like bits of insects, snails, and slugs. But be careful not to overfeed your pet.

The water in the aquarium should be kept clear and sweet-smelling all the time. Never keep your turtle in water that smells bad or looks cloudy or milky. Stale water will kill a baby turtle quickly.

In winter turtles will huddle in their shells. Move the turtle to a fairly dark, cool corner.

Turtles won't eat much in winter. If you keep their homes warm, they may come out for a swim and a bite to eat. But if the turtle does not eat the meal you have dropped into the tank, take it out. If you leave a meal in the aquarium too long, the water will become dirty. Dirty water will kill a turtle.

Turtles are clever. Some of them will come up to take things from your fingers. Some turtles will even let their heads be scratched. They may bend their heads way, way down so you can do a good job of scratching.

sweat

sweater

breath

leather

weather

heavy

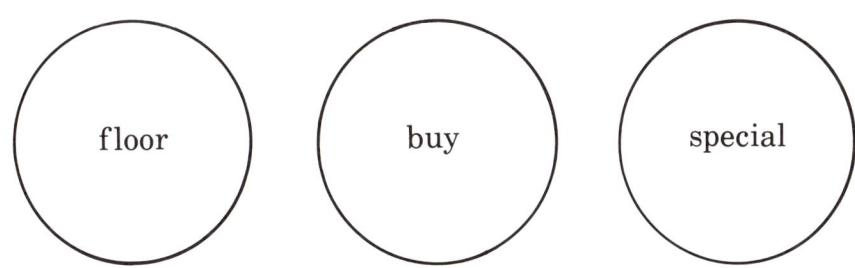

27

A Winter Day

It was a cold winter day. The people passing Jane's house looked frozen. Their cheeks and noses were red, and their breath came out in white puffs. Mrs. Banks came to stand near Jane at the window. They looked at the chilly people and at the trees bending in the wind.

At last Mrs. Banks said, "It's silly to let the weather keep us inside. If this were a school day, many families would send their children out, and I would send you, too. Let's get dressed in heavy clothes and go to Lane's Department Store. I read in yesterday's paper they are having a special sale."

So they got ready to go. But when Mrs. Banks turned the key in the car, the car didn't start.

"The battery must be dead," said Mrs. Banks. "It's this cold weather!" Then she said, "Well, we can always take the bus!"

The bus ride took a long time because several cars had stalled and were blocking the streets. When they got to Lane's, Jane wanted to look in the windows. But her mother said, "It's too cold out here. I'm sure Lane's has the same things inside."

On the first floor, Mrs. Banks looked for leather gloves. The special price of a pair with thick knitted linings was under ten dollars. "I'll buy these," Mrs. Banks said. She gave the salesclerk her credit card.

Jane and Mrs. Banks waited quite a while for the clerk to wrap the gloves. But at last the clerk came with the package. Then Mrs. Banks and Jane walked to the escalator. The customers on the escalator were all talking about the weather. They said the wind was much stronger, and it had begun to sleet. But Mrs. Banks still wanted to go to the sweater department on the third floor. She wanted to look at heavy sweaters for Jane.

One sweater with eight buttons was very nice. It was all red except for a bit of white trimming. But it wasn't the right size. The store had other red sweaters, but Jane didn't like any of them as well as the one that didn't fit.

"Well, let's buy some yarn. I can knit one like this for you instead," said Mrs. Banks.

Mrs. Banks was able to buy what she wanted in the yarn department. Nine balls of red yarn and one ball of white came to fifteen dollars. Mrs. Banks already had the special knitting needles for heavy yarn. She and Jane had to go to another floor for buttons.

Mrs. Banks said, "While we're here, I'll buy some thread since my supply is running short. Then we should start for home. People are saying the storm is terrible."

But on their way to the thread counter, they saw a boy who looked like Dan. Mrs. Banks said, "Did you tell me Dan's birthday is next week? We should buy his present today."

So after they got the thread, they went to the basement and got a sweat shirt for Dan.

Then Mrs. Banks said, "I really want to get home. I hope we won't have to wait for a bus!"

As they rode back up to the first floor, Jane said, "Mom, there's Uncle Russ! He's buying something at the shirt counter."

Just then Uncle Russ looked up and saw them. "Come here," he called, "and tell me if you like this shirt."

Mrs. Banks didn't really want to take the time, but she did. Uncle Russ was pleased when they said they liked the checked fabric of the shirt. As he paid for it, Uncle Russ asked, "Is your car parked on Lane's lot?"

"No," said Mrs. Banks, "we came by bus since our car wouldn't start. I think the battery is dead."

"Well," said Uncle Russ, "in that case, ride home with me! I'm ready to leave right away."

They were nice and warm in Uncle Russ's car. In a short time, Jane and her mother were delivered home safely. Mrs. Banks hugged Jane and said, "Wasn't that fun? I'm so glad we went!"

The Girl Who Wouldn't Give Up

Wilma Rudolph was born into a poor family. But it was a family rich in love. There were nineteen children in the family. Wilma was the seventeenth and the unlucky one.

When she was born, she weighed less than five pounds. From the start she was sickly. The doctors didn't think she would survive. Things didn't get better as she got older. When Wilma was sick with scarlet fever, her family didn't think she would live. But Wilma struggled through it. She was weak and tired much of the time, so she spent many days in bed. She wasn't able to run and play with her brothers and sisters.

Then Wilma was stricken with another disease, polio. Doctors said she would never walk. Wilma's parents would not accept that. They would not give up. Wilma had survived many things, and she would survive this.

Mrs. Rudolph took Wilma forty-five miles by bus to a special clinic. The doctors there examined Wilma. They ran tests. They poked and prodded and shook their heads. They weren't sure. Finally they told Mrs. Rudolph Wilma might be able to walk someday, but it would take a lot of hard work. Wilma's leg would have to be massaged every day. Mrs. Rudolph was concerned. She could not travel ninety miles every day to the clinic and back home. Perhaps she herself could be the one to massage Wilma's leg. The doctors showed her how. Mrs. Rudolph showed the older children how, too. They would all help Wilma.

Each day the family worked in shifts massaging Wilma's leg. Once a week Wilma would go to the clinic for special heat and water treatments. To Wilma it seemed as if someone were always massaging her leg. Sometimes she got tired of being fussed over and just wanted everybody to leave her alone. But Wilma did want to walk. She wanted to run and play like other children, so Wilma worked hard to be brave.

A year passed, and the doctors tested Wilma once more. There had been some improvement. The family was hopeful. If there had been some improvement, there could be more. Maybe one day Wilma would walk. They would just have to work harder.

By the time she was six, Wilma no longer had to sit and watch the other children play. She was playing with them! She could not walk yet, but she could hop. At first she fell a lot, but that didn't stop her. She would just get up and try over and over. And she kept on trying.

When Wilma was eight, the clinic gave her a leg brace. Wilma could limp with the brace. She grew stronger and stronger. By the time she was thirteen she was able to walk. Soon she was able to run, too!

Now Wilma could run and play with her brothers and sisters, and she loved every moment of it. It seemed as if she didn't ever want to stop running.

In school Wilma got on the girls' basketball team.

She was a good player. She buzzed all over the place, darting and dashing and dribbling the ball. She was so fast her coach gave her the nickname Skeeter. Soon everyone in school was calling her Skeeter. By the time she was fifteen, Skeeter was an all-state basketball player.

One day Ed Temple came to see her play. He wasn't interested in how many baskets she made. He was interested in how fast she ran. She was amazing!

"She could be a runner," he said, "a very good one."

Ed Temple was the track coach at Tennessee State University. He was so impressed with Wilma's speed and grace he invited her to try out for the women's track team. The team was called the Tigerbelles.

Wilma and her whole family were excited. If Wilma made the track team, she would get a college scholarship. How Wilma wanted to go to college and become a teacher! This was her chance. She knew she could do it. She had not given up hope in all those years when she was sick. She had worked hard then. She had overcome polio. She was not going to give up now. She would work hard and become a Tigerbelle.

Wilma went to the university that summer thinking she could do it—and she did. She made the track team, and she got her scholarship. She became a Tennessee State Tigerbelle.

In college Wilma kept working hard. She practiced running every day. Coach Temple helped her and urged her on. He was proud of her. He knew she could become a champion, and he was right. Soon Wilma became the fastest runner on the team.

In 1960 Wilma went to Rome, Italy, to compete in the Olympic Games. Sixty thousand people looked on and cheered for the spunky girl from Tennessee State. She was the favorite of the Olympics.

Wilma ran her best that day. She won three Olympic gold medals.

Everyone was proud of her. Her hard work had paid off. The sickly little girl had grown into a fast and graceful runner. Wilma Rudolph had become a winner.

wear
bear
tear
pear

busy
business

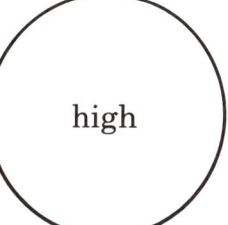
high

care	where	wear	wear
bare	wear	bear	where
bear	pear	tear	there

The First Plane Ride

Casey packed her bags slowly. She tried not to think about airplanes and flying and the butterflies inside her. She really wanted to be happy. She really should have been happy. After all she was going to visit her Aunt Kay in Dallas. The trip was a birthday gift from her mom and dad. It was just what Casey had wanted. What she didn't want was this airplane ride!

Casey had been nervous ever since the day Dad had given her the ticket. He had smiled and told her how exciting his first airplane flight had been. He was sure hers would be exciting, too. Casey wasn't so sure. Whenever she'd think about airplanes, she'd get butterflies inside. How she wished Mom and Dad were going with her!

Casey blinked. She had to stop this daydreaming and get the whole business of flying out of her head.

"Let's see," she said to herself. "What shall I wear? Something cheerful might help."

So Casey chose to wear her green and white print dress and her gold pear-shaped pin. She always felt happy when she wore that pin. But today it didn't work. She shook her head. She didn't feel happy. She just felt scared! She couldn't bear thinking about taking off in an airplane.

"Oh, this is silly!" Casey scolded herself. "People fly every day and love it. Surely it can't be so bad."

Casey took a deep breath, picked up her bags, and walked downstairs. Mom and Dad were waiting outside in the car.

On the way to the airport, Dad tried to reassure Casey. "There's not a thing to be afraid of, Case," he said. "Once you're up there, you'll love it!"

Casey sat quietly in the back seat. Her mouth was dry, and the butterflies had still not gone away.

Finally they arrived at the airport. It was busy today, very busy! People were everywhere. They were moving so fast. Too fast! Casey felt dizzy. Why wouldn't they stop? Why wouldn't they slow down?

Casey wanted to tear up her ticket. She wanted to turn around and run. She wanted to beg her mom and dad to take her back home. But more than all those things, she wanted to go to Dallas.

So Casey went to the ticket counter and checked her bags. Then she and her mom and dad went through the metal detector. After they had been cleared, they walked down a long, long corridor. Finally they came to Gate Eight.

Mom and Dad waited with Casey until it was time for her to get on the plane.

"Don't be so nervous," Mom said.

"Don't forget to write," Dad said, and he kissed Casey good-by. Then once more Dad assured her, "Case, you'll love it!"

Casey followed the line of passengers to the plane. Then slowly she walked up the steps and into the airplane.

Inside the plane Casey found her seat. She looked at the other passengers as they came into the plane.

Some were going on business trips, and some were going home. Some were going to visit, just as she was. But none of them, not one, seemed to be afraid.

As Casey stared out the window, she felt so alone. Suddenly the plane began to move. A flight attendant walked past and checked Casey's seat belt. The attendant smiled at her.

The plane jerked and began to move slowly down the runway. Casey looked out the window once more. Mom and Dad were waving and throwing good-by kisses. Casey hoped she wouldn't cry.

The plane began to move faster. The airport buildings became a blur as the plane sped past them. Casey could feel the plane lifting off the ground. Soon the people on the ground looked like little bugs. The buildings and cars looked smaller and smaller. The highways looked like little ribbons.

Up and up the plane flew. They were flying above the trees. Soon they were above the highest mountains. And higher still they flew. The land below soon faded from sight.

Suddenly they were flying through a soft white mist. It was like something in a dream. Then, just as suddenly, the sky was bright and clear. Casey smiled when she realized they were flying above the clouds! The clouds formed soft white hills below them like mounds of whipped cream.

Casey sat back and took a deep breath. She was still nervous, but she was happy, too. She had a tingly feeling inside. It was a strange feeling, but Casey was no longer scared. She was flying high above the mountains, high above the clouds. This was her first plane ride. It was thrilling. And, she loved it!

earth

earn

learn

early

month

won

wonder

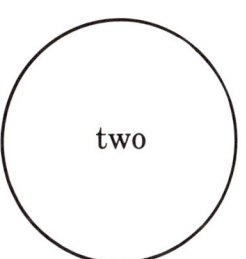
two

her
heard

turn
learn
earn

earn
earth
early

early
learn

A Basketball for Dan

Lots of people wear old clothes when they play. But Dan Bell could never remember to change his clothes after school. Someone always had to speak to him about it. If not, Dan just dropped his books anywhere and ran outside with Rags.

Early one evening Dan had just begun to study for a math test. He heard his dad call loudly from the living room, "Dan, please come here at once."

Mr. Bell was looking at the checkbook. He turned to Dan and said, "Dan, I know you tore another pair of slacks today. Last week you tore a pair when you fell off your bike. We'll have to buy you two new pairs of pants, so there won't be any money for a basketball this month. Dan, you must learn to take care of your clothes!"

Dan was upset. He was a good athlete, and he wanted a basketball more than anything. Besides that, he knew he would have to wear his best pants to school and be careful of them all day.

The next afternoon Dan and his dad went to Lane's Department Store. On the way Mr. Bell asked, "Did you do anything special in school today?"

"We had painting for the first time," Dan said. "But I was afraid I might get paint on these pants. So I had to use pencils instead."

"Oh, that was too bad," said Mr. Bell.

To get to boys' wear in Lane's, Dan and his dad had to walk through the sports department. Dan showed his dad two basketballs that were on sale.

"You'll get a basketball someday," said Mr. Bell. "But not right away. It would help if you could remember to change into old jeans for play."

The clerk smiled as Mr. Bell said, "I wonder if you have slacks made of something heavy like leather. My son tears the knees of all his pants."

"I've never heard of leather pants," the man said. "But we do have pants with leather patches on the knees. It seems strange to have patches on new clothes, but it really helps with torn knees."

Dan and his dad looked at the pants with the leather patches, but they didn't like them. At last Dan found a pair of pants he liked. Mr. Bell said, "They're very nice, Dan."

Mr. Bell knew Dan wished his package held a basketball instead of slacks. He said, "I know you'll try to make these pants last for a while. Then maybe we'll have the money for your basketball next month."

The next day Dan came right home after school. He set his books on the table and called to Rags. "Here, girl," he said, "let's go for a walk."

When Rags saw the leash, she knew she was going out. She was so happy she ran about until the leash was twisted around Dan's legs. When Dan looked down, he was still wearing his new pants.

"I wonder how long it will take me to learn," said Dan. Then he went upstairs, took off his new slacks, folded them neatly, and laid them on his bedroom chair. He changed his shirt and hung the good one on a hanger.

While Dan was walking Rags, he saw his mother. "Which pants are you wearing?" she asked.

"My old mended ones, Mom," said Dan.

"Wonderful!" said Mrs. Bell. "When I was in Lane's today, I found patches that look like denim. I'll press them over the mended spots on the pants you're wearing. That will give you two pairs of good pants for school."

A month later Mr. Bell left work very early. He drove into the yard just as Dan came home from school. As he took a large box from the car, he said, "Here, Dan, you've earned this. You learned to take care of your clothes, so you've won a prize!" It was a basketball!

Dan was excited! He began to bounce the basketball higher and higher on the hard earth of the yard. Then he stopped.

"What's wrong, Dan?" called Mr. Bell.

"I have to go change my clothes," said Dan. After that, no one had to tell Dan to change clothes.

Photo by Naismith Memorial Basketball Hall of Fame

The Peach-Basket Game
Mel Cebulash

Basketball! The Knicks and the Celtics play it. The Lakers and the Pistons play it. Boys and girls play it. They play it on teams. They play it alone. They play it in school gyms and in school yards. They play it in driveways and on street corners. Today basketball is played nearly everywhere by just about everyone. But how did the game get started?

Basketball started in 1891. The place was Springfield, Massachusetts. The head of the YMCA Training School had a problem with his students.

It was winter. The boys were not getting much exercise. Dr. James A. Naismith, the gym teacher, was asked to help. Could Dr. Naismith think of an indoor game for the boys?

One cold morning Dr. Naismith came to the gym with two peach baskets. He nailed one basket to the wall at one end of the gym. He nailed the other basket to the wall at the other end. The baskets were ten feet from the floor.

Adapted from *Basketball Players Do Amazing Things* by Mel Cebulash. Copyright 1976 by Mel Cebulash. With permission of Random House, Inc.

The eighteen students in the gym class wondered what Dr. Naismith was doing. They soon found out. Dr. Naismith divided the class into two teams of nine. Then he picked up a soccer ball. He said, "You are about to try a new game. It is really quite simple. One basket belongs to each team. You must try to get the ball into your basket, and the other team must try to stop you." Then Dr. Naismith told the teams a few other rules he had prepared.

"What is the name of the game?" one student asked.

Dr. Naismith looked at one of the baskets. Then he looked at the ball.

"I think I'll call it basketball," he said.

Moments later the first game of basketball began. The students liked the game. But they quickly learned that it was not easy. The game would take practice.

Dr. Naismith stood by a ladder. The baskets had no opening at the bottom. If the ball went into one of the baskets, it would stay there. Then Dr.

Naismith would have to go up the ladder and get the ball out. But he had to go up the ladder just once that morning. The final score of the first basketball game was one to zero.

Soon all the people in the school were taking shots at the peach baskets. And Dr. Naismith was preparing new rules for his game.

In 1892, Dr. Naismith published the rules for basketball. One rule was that the teams could have as few as three players. "But the more players, the more fun." However, no team was allowed to have more than forty players.

Today a basketball team has only five players. The ball is different, too. So are the baskets. And so is the name of the YMCA Training School. It is now Springfield College. But basketball is still about the same. Each team must try to score and stop the other team from scoring.

Dr. Naismith's game is now played by millions. And Springfield College—the place where it all started—is the home of the Basketball Hall of Fame.

Photo by Hank DeLespinasse/SPORTS ILLUSTRATED

find
kind
mind
wind

wild
mild
child

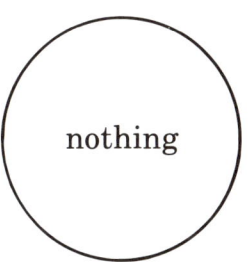

nothing

fine   mine   mile   mild
find   mind   mild   child
kind   wind   wild

Fishing for Fun

We all know people who like to fish. Fishing is just as much fun for a child as it is for an adult. If you want to do something that's lots of fun, find someone who will show you how to fish.

People fish in lakes, ponds, and brooks. They use fishing rods and reels. They may use different kinds of bait—a fly or a bit of raw fish or shrimp. Some people stand on a rock or sit in a boat. Some stand in the water to cast their lines. At the end of the line there is a hook with bait on it. When a fish nibbles on the bait the person winds in the line.

Some people fish at the seashore. They may just stand in the water or go out in small boats to fish. Others pay to fish from large boats that may hold as many as a hundred people. These boats go out as far as five miles from shore.

Each large boat has a captain or skipper. It's that person's business to steer the boat and to find schools of fish for the passengers. The captain has several helpers, but the captain is always in charge of the ship.

On some days the people on these large "party" boats may catch a lot of fish. On other days they may catch nothing at all.

Once in a while someone may catch a small shark or some other kind of fish that is not good to eat. Then the fish has to be tossed back. The hook must be baited for another try.

Sometimes some of the fishing lines on a big boat become tangled. The tangle is called a "bird's nest." The people try to untangle their lines. If they can't, they have to cut them, and the bird's nest falls into the sea. The fishhooks and heavy sinkers, or weights, don't cost a lot. But people have to buy others to replace the ones they have lost.

People who love fishing don't seem to mind whether they catch anything or not. Just being outdoors all day makes them happy. It's like a short vacation.

The Job of Catching Fish

Many people like to eat fish. When they go to the market to buy fish, they find many kinds. Some of it is fresh, some frozen, some dry, and some canned.

It takes planning and hard work by many people to supply all that fish. They have to catch different kinds in different ways. They may use fishing lines, nets, or traps.

Some fishing boats leave the dock at sunrise each morning and return each night. The people who work on that kind of boat get up while many of us are still asleep.

Another kind of fishing boat stays at sea for weeks at a time. The people who work on these boats have to eat and sleep on them. They may not see their families for as long as a month. They learn not to mind being away from home so long.

These people have to work in all kinds of weather. It's fine on mild days when the sun is shining and the sea is still. But strong winds can whip up high seas. Then they have to keep their minds on managing the boat so it doesn't turn over.

Finding and catching the fish is a big job. Small fish, such as smelts, swim in large numbers called schools. Nets are used to catch fish that travel in schools. One kind of net is used for fish that swim near the top of the water. Another kind of net is used for those that swim in deep water.

To catch big fish, many lines are thrown out with a hook on the end of each one. The hooks are baited with something the fish like to eat. When a fish is hooked, someone winds in the line on a big reel. This brings the fish close, so it can be lifted into the boat. If a fish fights to get free, the battle can be a wild one!

Many of the fish are cleaned right on the boat. Then they are packed in ice to keep them fresh. When the boat returns to the dock, some of the fish are packed in tin cans. Some are frozen. Some kinds of fish are rushed to markets so we can buy them while they are still fresh.

A Good Catch

Mark Benton's new job in Riverside was much better than his old one. After a while he was able to buy a new car.

But cars use a lot of gas, so Mr. Benton and his boss took turns driving to work. On two or three days each week, Mark rode with his boss, Bob Martin. On the other days Bob rode with Mr. Benton.

One morning traffic was very heavy as they drove across River Road Bridge. When all the cars came to a stop, Bob Martin had time to look way up the river. He saw a man fishing from a small boat.

"Would you like to go fishing this Saturday, Mark?" he asked. "I've just heard of a good place to try."

"That would be wonderful," said Mr. Benton. "There's nothing I'd like better, but I told Kim I'd help her with her batting this Saturday. She just loves baseball."

"Why don't you find time to play with her after dinner for the rest of the week?" asked Bob. "It's daylight until seven-thirty or eight o'clock these days."

"Good!" said Mr. Benton. "I'll see whether she's willing to do that."

So each night that week Mr. Benton pitched, and Kim worked hard at batting. Then on Saturday morning he was able to leave with his boss on the fishing trip. It was five o'clock, and the sun was just rising as the two of them drove away.

When they came back late that afternoon, the two men looked very happy. Jim, Kim, and Mrs. Benton rushed to look into the trunk of the car.

"This was our lucky day!" Bob Martin called to them. "The fish kept biting all day. Let me show you what I mean." He lifted the lid of the trunk. "There's not a fish under two pounds!"

"We had five or six more," said Mr. Benton, "but they were small, so we had to toss them back. The law says you can't keep a fish that is under a certain size. But we have plenty without the ones we tossed back."

"Did you clean some for dinner?" asked Mrs. Benton.

"Yes, I did, Sally," said her husband. "All they need is a hot frying pan."

"I'll carry them into the kitchen," said Jim, trying to lift the box.

"You'd better not try," said Bob Martin. "That big box of fish is packed with ice right to the top. You're quite strong, but I still think it's too heavy for you. I'll help."

So together Jim and Mr. Martin carried the box into the house. Bob took his share of the fish, and then he left. He wanted to get home in time for dinner with his wife and child.

When the fish were cooked, they tasted better than any that ever came from the market. The best part was they hadn't cost a penny! Just a day of work and fun.

put

push

pull
full

post
most
almost

(young)

rose / post / pull / full
pose / most / push / pull
post / almost / put / bull

A Team

Once when Ted was sick, a young doctor came to see him. Then Ted's mom had to go to the drugstore for medicine. A doctor and a druggist make a good team. They work together to make people well.

A doctor knows lots of ways to help sick people. Some new drugs may be used. The sick person may be given a shot or a prescription to be filled by the druggist. Most of the time the prescription is for pills the sick person must take several times a day.

Druggists are trained in college. They learn to read prescriptions. They have lots of big bottles and jars. These jars are filled with pills, capsules, and medicines.

First the druggist reads the prescription very carefully. There must be no mistakes. Then the medicine is put into a bottle. Next it is given to the person who has come for it. Or sometimes it is sent to the sick person's home.

A Fine Helper

Most of the people who live on Grove Street do their shopping in a big market near Ling Center. It has striped posts in front. It is called the Save-More Store.

The manager of the Save-More Store keeps the shelves full of canned goods, soap, scrubbing brushes, and lots of other things. There are good meats, young chickens, and fresh fish. And there is a dairy counter with milk, butter, and cheese. There is a drug department in the store, too.

Almost all the shoppers push their carts right past the drug counters. Instead they go to Mr. Farr's drugstore.

Mr. Farr's store is at the corner of Oak Street and Nineteenth Street. Near the front door are newspapers, magazines, and books for young people.

The next part of the store has shelves with hair sprays, cold cream, toothpaste, and shaving cream in cans and tubes. There are jars and tubes of makeup, also. The store is full of many things.

The most important part of the store is where Mr. Farr works as a druggist. When a customer comes in and hands him a prescription, Mr. Farr reads it carefully. Then he walks into his back room. Most of the time he pulls a jar from a shelf, counts out the right number of pills, and puts them into a bottle. Sometimes he has to mix different things to make the medicine the doctor has ordered. Then he comes out smiling and says, "I hope this will do the trick."

Mr. Farr has a helper, a high school girl named Jean. Jean works from three in the afternoon till the drugstore closes at ten. She waits on the customers, keeps the shelves full of goods, and does errands. She sweeps the floor, too. In winter she shovels the snow from the sidewalk.

One day Mr. Sands rushed in holding two prescriptions in his hand. "Can you fill these quickly?" he asked Mr. Farr. "Pam has a bad cold.

Dr. Young just examined her and gave me these to be filled. I'll take some ginger ale for her, too."

"Why don't you take the ginger ale and go home?" asked Mr. Farr. "It will take me a little while to get the medicine ready. Jean can deliver it to you later this afternoon."

"That's fine, Mr. Farr. I really don't want to leave Pam alone," said Mr. Sands.

At ten after three, Jean rang Mr. Sands's doorbell. When Mr. Sands came to the door, Jean said, "Here is Pam's medicine. Mr. Farr put a present in the package for her. Just call us if you want me to bring anything more."

"Thank you, Jean," said Mr. Sands. He took the package and closed the door. Then he went to Pam's room and helped her to sit up in bed. Mr. Sands filled a very small cup with medicine till it was almost full, but not quite. After Pam had taken the medicine, she fell asleep.

In the next five days Mr. Sands called the store several times. Once Pam needed more medicine. Then, when she began to feel better, she wanted a book of puzzles and some new pencils. Each time Jean took the things to Mr. Sands's house.

The last call was on a rainy day. Mr. Sands wanted something to rub on Pam's dry lips. When Mr. Sands called the druggist, he said, "It seems a shame to send Jean out in a rainstorm. Please wait till the storm blows over."

"Jean does not mind bad weather," said Mr. Farr. "And she does not like to make sick people wait. She'll be a good druggist some day."

"Yes," said Mr. Sands, "Jean will make a fine druggist. I thank both of you for being so helpful."

food
mood

moon
spoon

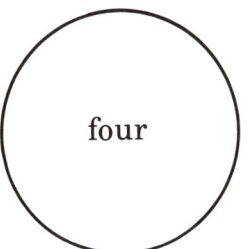
four

tool	moon	soon	spoon
moon	mood	moon	moon
mood	food	spoon	noon

On the Yellow Plains of Africa

It is a quiet night on the open plains of Africa.
The moon peeks from behind the clouds.
Soon you will see the silent herd.

Long necks extended upward—
    Shadows on the skyline.
    No movement. Not a sound.
They stand quietly, alert.

The moon drifts behind a cloud once more.
It leaves the herd in peaceful darkness.
The mood is like something from a dream.

They live on the open plains of Africa. Sometimes they are as tall as nineteen feet. Because their legs are so long, it would seem they'd be awkward creatures, but they are not. They are very graceful, gentle animals. And they are fast! Sometimes they move as fast as thirty miles an hour. They are the giraffes.

Male giraffes are called bulls. They are the tallest. Next are the female giraffes, which are called cows. Baby giraffes are the smallest, but even they stand more than five feet tall and weigh one hundred forty pounds. The long legs and necks of the giraffes are what give them their amazing height. A person could easily stand between a giraffe's front legs.

Giraffes eat the leaves from the thorn tree of Africa. They don't have to stretch their necks to reach the leaves. Hairs on their long lips protect them from the sharp thorns. To drink water from a stream or water hole, giraffes must bend their knees. Sometimes they straddle their front legs wide until their lips can reach the water.

Most of the time a giraffe swallows its food whole. It stores this unchewed food in one part of its stomach. Later it will bring the food back into its mouth to chew it. Bringing the food back up is called "chewing the cud." Cattle, sheep, and deer chew their cuds, too. They all have four parts to their stomachs. One part is used to store the food. The other three parts are used to digest the food after it has been chewed.

You might think giraffes are silent animals. People used to think giraffes couldn't make any sounds, but a giraffe cow has been heard to call to her baby in a sort of "mooing" sound.

Slowly the giraffes move about in their herds. Silently, they nibble on the leaves of the trees. They flick their ears and twitch their noses. They swing their long slender necks.

It is quiet and peaceful on the yellow plains of Africa.

Dr. Jenson's Tall Problem
Ann Elwood

Debby Jenson had loved animals since she was just four years old. So when she grew up, she went to college to become a veterinarian, or animal doctor. Studying had been hard. It had taken many years, but at last she could call herself Dr. Jenson. Now she could examine sick animals. She could tell what was wrong with them and treat them to make them well. She could even operate on them.

Late one afternoon Dr. Jenson was feeding a very sick dog from a spoon. The dog had just eaten the last spoonful of food when a call came.

"Doctor," said the man on the other end of the line, "I have a problem." He seemed nervous.

"What is it?" asked Dr. Jenson.

"It's hard to explain," the man said. "Maybe you could come and see for yourself. I'm in the lot near the firehouse."

"All right," answered Dr. Jenson. "I'll drive over and take a look."

When Dr. Jenson got near the lot, she saw a big banner hanging above the street. It said, "Sandy's Circus." Dr. Jenson smiled to herself—a circus animal to treat!

Just then a man came running up to her car. "Are you the doctor?" he asked. Without waiting for an answer, he led Dr. Jenson to the back of the lot. A giraffe stood there. "Something's wrong with Ginny's ear," the man said.

"Let me see," Dr. Jenson said. She looked puzzled. "I can certainly treat her ear if I can get to it. I think I'll need a ladder."

"We don't have a ladder that long," the man said. He looked very tense. "Without Ginny, the circus can't go on!"

"Now don't upset yourself," said Dr. Jenson. "There's got to be a way. Just let me think a second." A frown wrinkled Dr. Jenson's forehead. Suddenly her face lit up. She snapped her fingers and said, "I know! The fire department has a long ladder. Maybe we can use it!"

It didn't take long for the fire department to bring a ladder to the lot. The fire fighters all waited to see Dr. Jenson go up the ladder. At last the doctor was on her way up to Ginny's ear.

Dr. Jenson went to the top of the ladder. As she reached for Ginny's head, Ginny moved her neck away. Dr. Jenson reached a second time. Once more the giraffe moved her neck. Ginny moved her neck too far and too fast for Dr. Jenson. How could Dr. Jenson put medicine into Ginny's sore ear?

"I've got to try something else," said Dr. Jenson as she came down the ladder. "I'll do what I'd do with any other frightened animal. What does Ginny like to eat?" she asked the owner.

"Leaves," said Ginny's owner, and he ran to get some.

A little later the vet went back up the ladder, carrying leaves in one hand and medicine in the other. Then she began talking in a soft, gentle way.

"Come here, Ginny," she sang. "I've got some nice leaves for you, and I'll make you well. It will be all right." She held out the leaves.

Ginny turned and looked at the leaves. She moved her head near Dr. Jenson's hand. Dr. Jenson kept talking. At last Ginny stuck out her long lips, reached over, and took a leaf. Quickly Dr. Jenson put her arm around the giraffe's neck and put the medicine into Ginny's ear. Ginny held still. She seemed to know the veterinarian was a friend.

When Dr. Jenson came down the ladder, Ginny's owner was grinning. "I'm so grateful to you," he said.

"Oh, I like strange problems," said Dr. Jenson. She looked up the ladder. "I'm just glad I didn't have to operate on that ear from this ladder. That really would have been too hard!"

toot

boot

root

groove

roof
proof

again

too	toot	root	groove
toot	boot	roof	prove
tooth	booth	proof	proof

Music in the Home

Mrs. Benton was in a sad mood. Something was wrong with one of her teeth. Her jaw hurt too, and she hadn't slept a wink all night. She kept thinking she might have to have the tooth pulled if the root were bad. At last she called the dentist and told him about the pain.

The dentist said, "You sound as if you have a cold, too. Maybe that's why your jaw feels sore. Come in on Thursday, and I'll take some X-rays."

Another thing that made Mrs. Benton unhappy was the rain. It had been raining hard for three days. On the second rainy day the roof had begun to leak. The Bentons couldn't get it fixed right away, so Mrs. Benton put a pail under the leak. She had to empty the pail over and over again.

Then on the third day Jim had walked into a deep puddle on his way home. He had come in with his boots full of water and his slacks wringing wet. Besides that, Kim had lost her purse. And one of the clerks in Mrs. Benton's shop had been sick for days.

That night Mrs. Benton told her husband all that had happened. She finished by saying, "It might not have been so bad, Mark, if I hadn't had to empty the rainwater out of that bucket again and again. I already have too many things to do."

"Well," said Mr. Benton, "I'll take care of emptying the bucket tonight. We'll get the roof fixed as soon as it stops raining."

Just then a new sound filled the room. "Root-a-toot-toot," it went. It was Kim's flute.

"You'd better not play your flute while your mom isn't feeling well," Mr. Benton called to Kim.

"I have to, Dad," said Kim as she came into the room. "We have to play in an assembly on Thursday."

"Let her play, Mark," said Mrs. Benton. "It may take my mind off this tooth!"

Kim began practicing the five songs the band was

going to play. As she played the last one, her mother started humming the tune. At the end she said, "Isn't that the music from 'Hansel and Gretel'? We have it on one of our records. Mark, where are the records? I know we haven't unpacked them yet."

Mr. Benton put down the mail he was reading. "I'll look for them," he said.

He went to the closet and pulled out a box. Soon he said, "Here it is—'Hansel and Gretel.'"

He put the record on the turntable, started the record player, and put the needle in the first groove. Very soon the sound of music filled the house.

"That's the same song Kim was playing," said Jim.

"Yes, it is," said Mrs. Benton as she kept time with the music. Then she said, "It's time for dinner. I'll put the food on the table. Let's eat with the music playing!"

Soon the family felt better. The music had put the Bentons back into a good mood.

The First Music

When some people are upset, music seems to make them feel better. The same thing has happened to people since music was first played.

People have always had some kind of music. First it was the songs of birds. Then someone pulled up the hollow stem of a plant and blew into it. That may have been the first musical instrument.

But some people think the first music was made when early people beat on a hollow log. Others say people made the first music by stamping their feet or slapping their hands against their bodies.

We do know that people of very long ago made music of some kind. They used drums, rattles, and pipes. We now call some of those pipes flutes. Such musical instruments have been dug up in spots where people lived many hundreds of years ago. They are taken as proof that the people of those times had some kind of music.

Later on people began to make up songs and to

sing them. They did not have a way to write down the ones they liked best. They didn't have records, record players, or tape recorders. Still they kept the songs alive by singing them. Parents sang songs to their children. Later, when these children were mothers and fathers, they sang the same songs to their own children.

At last a way to write music was invented. Then there was less danger of forgetting the songs.

Some music is still written just to be sung. Some is written to be sung and to be played on instruments at the same time. Some of it is to be played by many instruments at once.

We still have flutes and drums. But we have other wind instruments as well as flutes. For example, the trumpet, the bugle, and the French horn are all played by blowing into them. We have other instruments besides drums that are played by striking them. That's how the kettle drum and the marimba are played. You can hear all these at concerts, on records and tapes, and on TV.

owl
howl
fowl
prowl
growl

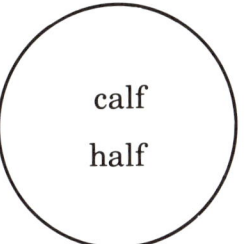

calf
half

how	now	growl	fowl
howl	prowl	prowl	howl
fowl	growl	owl	how

A Night To Remember

One Saturday morning in September, Ms. Perez said to her husband, "Vince, let's go to the lake tomorrow. It's the last weekend Carlos will be home. His classes at college start next Wednesday, you know."

"That's fine with me," said Mr. Perez. "We can get some of the things ready tonight. But hitching up the boat trailer will have to wait until morning. Carlos wants to use the car tonight."

Eight-year-old Rosa, who was listening, was delighted. Driving to Lake Mead was fun. She always took Jack, her dog, with her. They sat in the back seat because Jack was such a frisky dog. It wasn't safe to have him in front with the driver.

Sometimes Mom drove the car and sometimes Dad drove. It all depended on which one was in the mood. When Carlos went along, he always wanted to drive. His parents often let him take the wheel.

When Sunday morning came, Carlos was too sleepy to drive. Half awake and half asleep, he sat in the back of the car with Rosa. He did not even want to play a car game his sister liked.

So, after a minute, Rosa asked her parents to play the game with her. She said, "I am thinking of a bird that can see at night."

"Is it an owl?" asked Ms. Perez.

"That's right," said Rosa. "Now it's your turn."

"All right," said Ms. Perez. "Put a letter in front of *owl* and get a hen or a chicken."

"A rooster?" asked Carlos, trying to wake up.

"No," said his father. "You'd better go back to sleep. It's a fowl. Now it's my turn. Use another letter instead of the *f* in *fowl*. It's the sound a dog might make when it sees a full moon."

"I know that one," said Rosa. "It's *howl*. Now I'll give you another sound. Jack does this when he sees a stranger."

"Is it *growl*?" asked Carlos.

"Good for you, son!" said Mr. Perez. "That proves you're awake!"

Everyone was still for a little while. Then Ms. Perez slowed the car a bit. "All those questions remind me of a night long ago," she said. Then she told this story.

It was on our little farm when I was about your age, Rosa. I woke up suddenly, as if someone had called to me. I heard an owl hoot. Then our dogs began to growl. The horses were restless, too. I heard Tomas, our cow pony, neighing.

Our chickens began to cackle. I had never heard fowl cackle in the middle of the night.

I went to my parents' room and woke my father. I said, "Papa, something has wakened all the animals. Perhaps some wild animal is prowling around. Perhaps someone has got into our barn."

My father pulled on his pants over his nightshirt.

"You are a good farmhand," he said. Then he went to the kitchen and got his big lantern. My mother came to the kitchen, too.

The three of us went to the barn together. We were very happy when we looked around. Minna, our best cow, was licking a newborn calf. Soon it would stand on its wobbly legs.

My father told me, "All the animals were awake to welcome the new calf. It is a lucky night for all of us."

A City Map

Look at the map on page 89. Then use it to answer these questions.

1. What streets surround the park?
2. On which street is the museum located?
3. Kathy lives at the corner of which streets?
4. Is the shopping center on the north or the south side of town?
5. What three ways can Kathy get to school?
6. What is one way to get from the school to the hospital?
7. Is the museum on the east or the west side of town?
8. If you lived on Dobbs Drive, how might you get to the shopping center?
9. Start at the corner of South Second and Liberty. Go west on Liberty to Main. Make a right onto Main. Go to Franklin. Make a right onto Franklin. Stop at the corner of Franklin and Hays. What building have you come to?

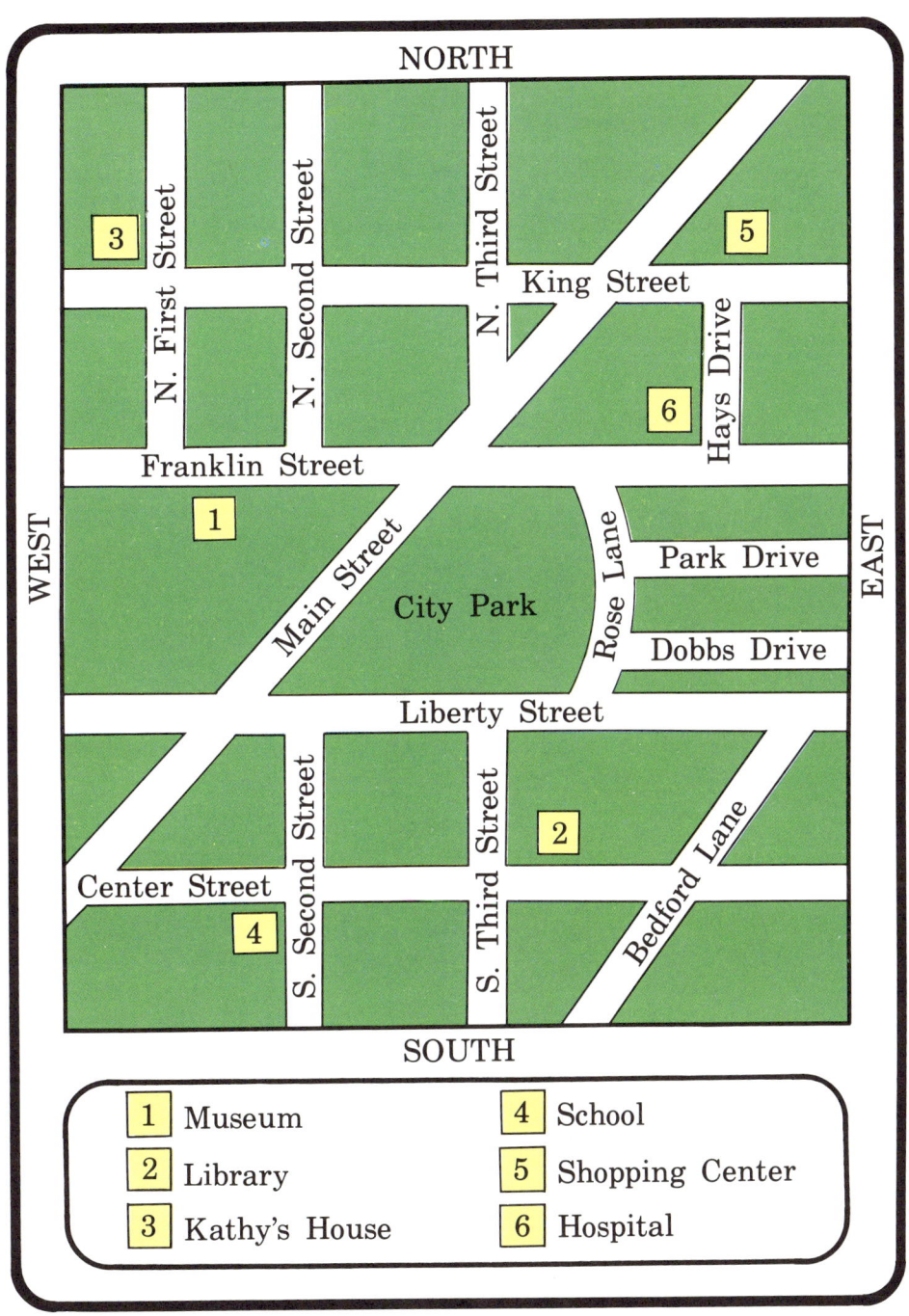

My Teacher and I

My teacher said, "Now write a poem
That shows how you would feel
If you were an ice cream cone
Or an electric eel."

Now I can't think this is for real.
I can't even pretend.
A cone? An eel? An eight-line poem?
Aha! This line's the end!

Illustration by Carol Newsom

chief
thief
grief
belief
relief

believe
relieve

beef	leaf	chief	believe
leaf	belief	thief	relieve
chief	relief	grief	relief

Life on a Ranch

One day when Beth and Dom Santis came home from work, Red was waiting for them, "What a relief to see you!" said Red. "You're late, and I was getting concerned."

"Traffic was heavy, and I was late leaving work. Good grief!" said Beth as she looked at the kitchen clock. "It's past seven!"

"Well, I'm relieved you're here," said Red. "I'll call the children."

When the family sat down for dinner, Red said, "I had a letter today."

Kathy said, "Who wrote to you?"

"The family I worked for before I came here," said Red. "They have had a good year and wanted to tell me all about it. It made me start thinking of life on the ranch."

Everyone tried to talk at once. Red was asked a

hundred different things. The children already knew half the answers, but they kept Red busy telling them everything once more.

"Yes," he said, "a cowpuncher's chief job is to keep the cattle together on the range. That's exactly what I used to do. I also had to search for water holes and feeding places."

"Did you have to brand any cattle?" Dom asked.

"More than I can count," said Red. "By the way, don't believe that old story that a cattle thief can change a brand. It's my belief that a good cowhand can always tell if a new brand has been stamped on top of an old one. You can trace both of them."

Bill and Kathy were more interested in hearing about the children in the King family. "How old are those children now?" Bill asked. "Are they as big as we are? Where do they go to school? Do they have horses?"

"Did you play the fiddle for them, too?" Kathy wanted to know.

Manny wanted to hear about campfires and wild animals. They all liked to hear about roping and branding. And they asked about cattle rustlers.

They had asked Red all of these things each time there was a western on TV. But they all liked to hear the stories over and over.

They knew cowhands have to protect their herd from thieves. But Red told them there was one thing all cowhands fear more than stealing.

He said, "Cowhands believe a stampede is more of a danger than a cattle thief. A stampede can be started by almost anything. The howl of a wild animal can start a stampede. So can the sound of thunder. Even the smell of water in the middle of a dry spell can make the cattle stampede."

Then Red went on, "A stampede can be started by just one animal. It begins to run. Then all the others follow. They must be stopped before they trample each other to death or plunge over a cliff."

"Oh, that's exciting," said young Kathy. "I know

what I'm going to be when I grow up—a ranch hand."

"Don't forget how hard you'll have to work," said Red.

"I bet the other cowhands would be happy to see you come back to help with all that hard work," said Kathy. "They would be down at the train platform, ready to pound you on the back. They would all yell, 'Welcome back, Red!'"

"No, they wouldn't," said Red, smiling.

"What do you mean?" asked Dr. Santis. "I know they would all love to have you come back."

Dom was looking at Red. He was puzzled to think Red might not be welcome back on the King ranch. "Why would they write you such a nice letter if they wouldn't be glad to see you?" he asked.

"Oh, they'd be glad to see me," said Red, "but they wouldn't call me Red."

"What did they call you?" asked Beth.

Dom Santis remembered Red's real name on the letter from Mr. King. He knew it was Jeff. "Please explain why you have two names," he said.

"Well," said Red, "when I meet people for the first time, they see my red hair before they see anything else. They begin to call me Red right away. That's been my nickname since I was in first grade."

He went on, "But that didn't happen when I went to work on the King ranch. The people there had been trying for a year to catch a big wild red horse. They had named the horse Red, so they couldn't call me Red. People might not know which one of us they were talking about. So they called me Jeff, which is my real name. I was glad when you started calling me Red from the start. It's the name I'm used to."

"I could never think of you by any name but Red," said Kathy.

oil
boil
soil
spoil
broil

join
joint
point
appoint

noise

idea

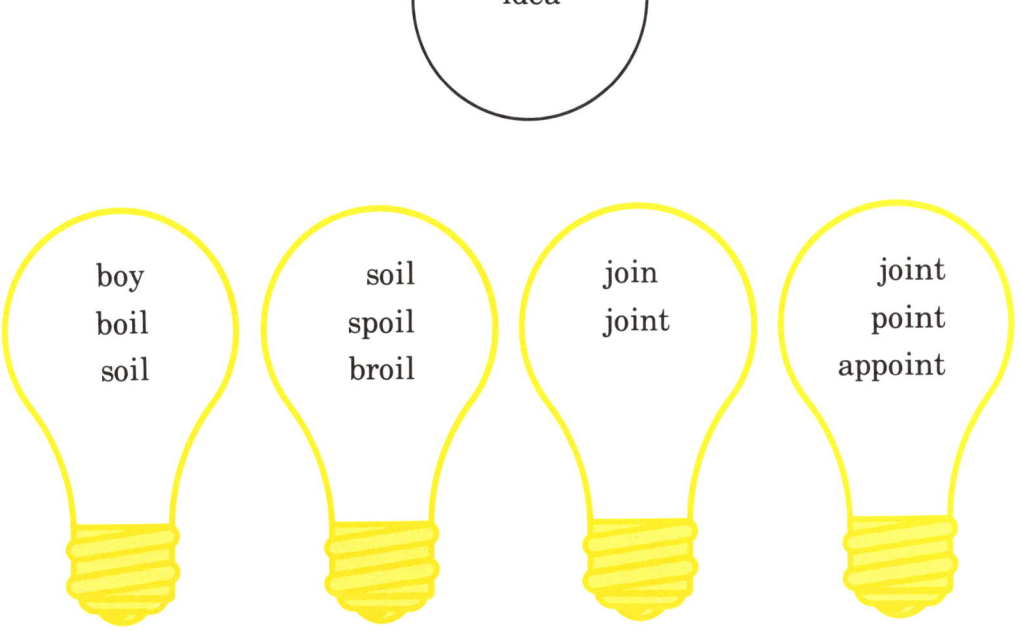

Dinner for All

At two o'clock one rainy Sunday afternoon, the Bells were in the living room. Dan and Jan were reading the paper. Mrs. Bell was trying to find a baseball game on TV. Grandma Smith had come for Sunday dinner. She was playing chess with Mr. Bell.

"I know there's a game in Bay City today," Mrs. Bell said. She turned from one channel to another. "It's supposed to be on TV."

"It may be raining there, too," said Mr. Bell. Just then the phone in the kitchen rang. Dan answered it.

"Dad," he said, "it's Uncle Dave. He's calling from Bay City. There's so much noise at his end I can hardly hear."

Mr. Bell said, "That's odd. I wonder what Dave's doing in Bay City."

Mr. Bell went to talk with his brother. When he returned to the living room, he looked pleased. "There's nothing wrong," he told them. "Dave drove to Bay City with his family to see the game, but it's been rained out. They're disappointed their day has been spoiled. Then I had an idea. I invited Dave to come here for a visit. I suppose the drive will take at least an hour."

"I hope you asked them to join us for dinner," said Mrs. Bell.

"Yes, I did," said Mr. Bell.

By this time Dan and Jan were very excited. "Mom," said Dan, "may I sit next to Anthony at the dinner table?"

"And I'd like to sit between Polly and Eddy!" said Jan. "Kenny can be across from me."

Then Mrs. Smith got up from her chair. "What can I do to help?" she asked.

"Wow!" said Mrs. Bell. "There will be eleven of us

for dinner instead of five. Everyone will have to help." Soon each member of the family had one special thing to do.

"Tom," she said, "will you make the iced tea?"

"Sure," said Mr. Bell. "I'll just boil some water and put in some tea bags. We'll probably need two pitchers."

"Jan," said Mrs. Bell, "please pick up all the things on the living room floor. Fold the Sunday papers and save them. Dan, put some little crackers in one dish and a lot of pretzel sticks in another. Then you and Jan are appointed to set the table."

Then Mrs. Smith said, "Dot, will you shell the peas? I'll cut some carrots to put with them. It's lucky we are having broiled chicken. It doesn't take long, and it's always good. I saw some chickens thawing in the sink. But we'll need more."

Mrs. Bell didn't want to soil the outfit she was wearing. She went to her bedroom and changed into a sweater and slacks. When she came back, she took four more packages of chicken from the freezer.

The chickens had already been cut apart at the joints. So Mrs. Bell just spread them out near the stove. "By the time I finish broiling the first batch, these will be nearly thawed," she said.

While Mrs. Bell broiled the chicken, Mr. Bell made the salad dressing. He put oil, vinegar, salt, and pepper into a glass jar and shook it hard. "This dressing is always good on wedges of lettuce," he said. "It doesn't spoil the fresh taste of the lettuce."

"Look at that!" said Mrs. Bell. She pointed to Dan, who was fixing the pretzels.

Dan was eating more pretzel sticks than he was putting into the dish. His mom took the box from him. "That's not a good idea, Dan," she said. "You'll spoil your appetite. If you're full of pretzels, you won't have room for chicken."

"Well, chicken's better than pretzels," said Dan. He took the dish into the living room.

When Uncle Dave's car pulled up in front of the house, dinner wasn't quite ready. It was a good thing the food needed a little more cooking time.

Aunt Hilda and young Polly had raincoats. But Uncle Dave and the boys got soaked as they ran from the car to the house. Mrs. Bell ran for towels to dry their wet hair. Mr. Bell got dry shirts for his brother and the three boys.

At last they sat down for dinner. There were two big platters of broiled chicken. They had rice with mushrooms, green peas and carrots, a salad with homemade dressing, and iced tea, too. In a short time the food was all gone.

As they finished eating, Uncle Dave said, "I've never been so pleased to have a ball game rained out!"

Aunt Hilda said, "Everything was just perfect! I don't see how you did it!"

The Bells smiled and said, "Oh, it's easy when everyone pitches in!"

Let's Make a Salad

BEFORE YOU MAKE THIS SALAD, STOP!

Are you allowed to work in the kitchen by yourself?
Do you know how to use a table knife to slice a banana?
Do you have everything listed below?
If you answered YES to all the questions, you may begin.

<u>You will need:</u>

1 banana

1 bunch of grapes

1 orange

10 strawberries

½ cup of plain yogurt

1 tablespoon of honey

1 tablespoon of orange juice

a bowl

a wooden mixing spoon

a tablespoon

a measuring cup

a table knife

Illustration by Holly Zapp

READ THESE NINE STEPS BEFORE YOU BEGIN.

1. Peel the banana. Throw away the peel. Slice the banana, and drop the slices into the bowl.
2. Wash the grapes by running warm water over them. Remove the grapes from the stalk, and drop them into the bowl. You can throw away the stalk.
3. Peel the orange. Throw away the peel. Pull the orange sections apart and drop into bowl.
4. Wash the strawberries by running warm water over them. Pull off the stems. Throw the stems away. Drop the strawberries into the bowl.
5. Measure exactly ½ cup of plain yogurt. Put this yogurt on top of the fruit in the bowl.
6. Measure exactly one tablespoon of honey. Pour the honey over the yogurt.
7. Measure exactly one tablespoon of orange juice. Add it to the fruit, yogurt, and honey.
8. Now use the wooden mixing spoon to stir the mixture carefully. Be sure that all the fruit, yogurt, honey, and orange juice are well mixed.
9. You and three friends can now share your salad!

toy

employ

annoy

destroy

great

break

steak

eye

boy	joy	enjoy	steak
toy	enjoy	annoy	break
joy	employ	destroy	great

The Toy Sale

"Hi, Grandpa!" yelled Jay Sung and Sue Lin.

"Hello," said Grandpa. "How was school?"

"OK. What's for dinner?" Jay Sung asked.

"Steak," said Grandpa without turning around.

"Great!" Jay Sung said. He loved steak!

"I hate steak," Sue Lin grumbled.

Jay Sung and Grandpa looked at each other and shook their heads. "She's always complaining about something," Jay Sung said.

When Jay Sung and Sue Lin had washed their hands and sat down, Grandpa said, "Your mother is working late. And I'll be going out for a while. Jay, you will have to keep an eye on Sue Lin."

"Grandpa," Jay Sung pouted, "she's six years old! Can't she keep an eye on herself?"

"Jay Sung, you have to help around here, too," said Grandpa.

"I know, Grandpa," said Jay Sung. "I'm really sorry." Then to break the silence, Jay Sung said, "Are you going swimming tonight?"

"No, I'm going for a walk," Grandpa said softly.

"I enjoy walking," Grandpa said when he saw their puzzled stares.

"But, Grandpa, you always go to the swim club on Friday," Sue Lin said.

Jay Sung was confused. "Grandpa, you don't enjoy walking as much as you enjoy swimming. Why aren't you going to the swim club?"

Finally Grandpa said, "I didn't renew my membership. We need the money for other things. It's not going to destroy me if I don't go swimming every Friday. I don't want to talk about it any more. I'll be back soon. Sue Lin, try not to annoy your brother too much." Then he smiled, winked an eye at them, and left.

"I'll help with the dishes," Sue Lin offered. She didn't want to annoy Jay Sung.

"Thanks," said Jay Sung. "You know, it isn't fair for Grandpa to give up his swimming. He enjoys it."

"He thinks we need the money," Sue Lin said.

"We can do just fine without it," said Jay Sung.

"If I could just get a job," Jay Sung said to himself. But there weren't many places that would employ a twelve-year-old. Besides, there was school. And he had to keep an eye on Sue Lin. Then his eyes widened, and a smile spread across his face.

"I think I know what we can do," he said to Sue Lin. And he told her his plan.

The next morning Jay Sung and Sue Lin quietly carried boxes of toys and a table out of their apartment. Then just as they were going out with a large sign, their mother came into the room.

"Good morning," she said. "You two have been busy this morning. What's going on?"

"We've got a plan," Jay Sung whispered. Then he and Sue Lin told their mother everything.

"Please don't tell Grandpa," they said.

Mom smiled. "I'm proud of you, and Grandpa will be happy. But are you sure you want to do this?"

"We're sure," they said as they left the room.

In front of the apartment building the children set up their table. They placed the smaller toys on it and the larger ones on the lawn. Jay Sung taped the sign to the table. It said this: Big Toy Sale.

Sue Lin and Jay Sung had told all their friends about the toy sale. But after an hour of waiting, they were afraid no one was going to come. At last their first customer arrived. Finally she took three comic books. Soon other people came, and by noon Jay Sung and Sue Lin had sold almost everything.

Mom came downstairs. "Aren't you going to take a break for lunch?" she asked.

"Mom, we still have things to sell," said Sue Lin. But Mom handed Jay Sung another sign. This one said Out to Lunch. Jay taped it to the table, picked up the toys, and went upstairs.

After lunch Sue Lin whispered to Jay Sung, "Let's count the money. Maybe we have all we need."

Jay Sung agreed, and they went into his room. Soon Mom knocked on the door and came in. "How did you do?" she asked.

"We need ten more dollars," Jay said sadly, "and all we have left is junk."

"Wait right here," Mom said. She returned with a ten dollar bill. "I'd like to buy a box of junk," she said as she handed the money to Jay Sung.

They looked at each other for a moment. Then they all smiled as Jay Sung handed Mom the box.

The next Friday Jay Sung and Sue Lin gave Grandpa a new swim club membership card.

"I've never felt such joy," Grandpa said. And he smiled at the family he was so proud of.

Illustration by Kinuko Craft

Falling Snow

See the lovely snowflakes
Falling from the sky.
On the walk and housetop
Soft and thick they lie.

On the window ledges,
On the branches bare,
Now how fast they gather,
Filling all the air.

Look into the garden,
Where the grass was green.
Covered by the snowflakes,
Not a blade is seen.

Now the bare black bushes
All look soft and white.
Every twig is laden—
What a lovely sight!

Illustration by Kinuko Craft

ought
fought
brought
thought

caught
taught
naughty
daughter

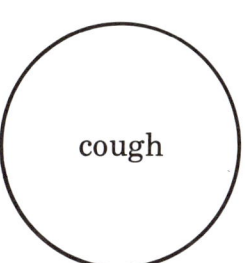

cough

taught	fought	caught	fought
thought	bought	naughty	brought
brought	brought	daughter	thought

The Lesson

My plan certainly backfired! This morning I faked a cold so I could stay home from band practice. Was that ever a mistake!

When Mom heard me cough, she said, "I think you're catching a cold. You ought to stay home today."

Well, that's just what I wanted to hear. After Mom left for work, I got dressed and turned on the TV. When the ten o'clock game show was over, I got up to change the channel. That's when it all began. I stumbled and knocked Mom's new vase off the table. It crashed to the floor and broke into big ugly chunks.

"I'll have to buy her another one," I said to myself. "Mom loved that vase."

I counted all my money, hoping I had at least ten dollars. But I had only nine dollars and thirty cents. Then I remembered my penny jar. I had been saving pennies for a year. I grabbed the jar and carefully counted two hundred and ten pennies. That would pay for the vase and my bus fare.

I picked up my purse, ran out the door, and headed for the bus stop. I almost missed the bus, but the driver saw me waving and yelling. He stopped and waited for me.

On the bus I counted out fifty pennies and dropped them into the coin box. The driver probably thought I was crazy!

When the bus got downtown, I got off and headed for Joy's Department Store. I fought my way through the crowd and ran all the way to the third floor. I looked around and saw a vase just like Mom's. Carefully I took it to the counter to pay for it.

"That will be twelve dollars and forty cents," said the salesclerk.

"But my mom bought the same kind of vase here last week for ten dollars!" I said.

"Last week these vases were on sale," she said.

Now what could I do? Mom would be so upset. There was just one thing left to do.

I dashed down the stairs and fought my way through the crowd again. I stepped inside the revolving doors. Just as I was coming out of the doors, I slipped and fell. My purse flew into the air. I looked at the sidewalk, which was now covered with pennies. "I ought to be more careful!" I thought.

I picked up as many pennies as I could find. Then slowly I went to the five-and-dime and bought a jar of rubber cement.

By the time I got home I was tired! I was wet and cold! And I was angry with myself!

I had been more than just a naughty daughter this time. I mended Mom's vase with the cement and decided right then to tell her everything. Everything I had done was wrong!

When Mom came home, I said, "Mom, your new vase is broken, and I—"

"I know," Mom interrupted. "I broke it the day after I bought it. But I put it together with some rubber cement."

"YOU broke it?" I gasped. "Oh, no!" Then I told her the whole story. And I started to sneeze and sniffle and cough. I really had caught a cold.

"Well, you really have been a naughty daughter today," said Mom. "And now you have caught a real cold on top of everything. So get yourself into bed. I hope this has taught you a lesson!"

"Believe me, it has!" I said. "I'll never do anything like this again. And I'm sorry I tried it today."

Mom just brought me some chicken broth. Do I hate chicken broth! But I learned my lesson! Never again will I pretend to be sick!

In the News Today

CONTENTS

Arts	14	Letters	5
Books	16	Movies	11
Business	24	Radio-TV	19
For Sale	22	Sports	26
Gardening . . .	18	Travel	27
Jobs	20	Weather	6

In this newspaper, where would you look to find the answers to these questions?

1. What movies are playing?
2. How many people want to hire taxi drivers?
3. When is the best time to plant roses?
4. How much might a 1973 car cost?
5. What was last night's basketball score?
6. Was your letter to the editor printed today?
7. On which channel can the football game be seen tonight?
8. Will it be cold tomorrow?

rough
tough
enough

word
worry
worse
worst
worth

beautiful

earth   work   enough   enough
worth   word   rough   tough
worse   worry   tough   rough

The Golden Touch

Long ago there lived a very rich king named Midas. He loved only one thing more than gold, his daughter Marygold.

King Midas kept his gold locked in the basement of his palace. Each day he went there to count his coins. He had lots of gold, but he wanted more.

One day as Midas counted his treasure, a stream of light came into the room. It was like a golden sunbeam. Midas looked up to see a handsome stranger. He had a cheerful face that lit up the whole room. The heaps of gold sparkled more than ever. He gazed about the room.

"You are indeed a wealthy man, King Midas," the young stranger said.

"Oh, this is just a small amount," said King Midas. "It took me a lifetime to save only this much."

"Is this not enough?" the stranger asked.

"Not nearly enough," Midas said sadly.

"And what would please you?" asked the stranger.

Midas thought a long time. He imagined all the gold in the world. He imagined it all belonged to him. But it would take him forever to collect it all. And where could he store so much gold? This was a tough problem for Midas. Then he had an idea.

"I would be so happy," he told the stranger, "if everything I touched turned to gold."

"Would that be enough for you?" the stranger said.

"Oh, yes!" said Midas. "What could be better than to have the golden touch?"

"Well, you shall have it," said the stranger. "Tomorrow at sunrise you shall have the golden touch."

Then the room lit up so brightly Midas had to close his eyes. When he opened them, the room was dark again. The sunbeam and the stranger were gone. King Midas wasn't sure what to think. Had he imagined the stranger? Would he really be granted his wish at sunrise?

That night Midas could not sleep. He was so afraid he had just dreamed about the stranger. He wanted the night to end so he would know if he had been given the golden touch.

At last morning came. Midas sat up. He could hardly wait to see if the stranger had kept his word. Midas began to touch everything. Nothing happened! Poor Midas! He thought this was the worst day of his life. He began to grow very sad.

Then the first ray of sunlight shone through the window. Midas looked down at his blankets. The spread was now a bright sparkling gold! Midas was delighted! The golden touch had come to him with the first sunbeam of the day.

Midas ran around the room touching everything, and each thing he touched turned to gold. He opened the curtains. They turned to gold. As Midas dressed, the clothes he put on were also turned to gold. They were heavy and quite rough to wear, but that didn't bother Midas. He had the golden touch!

As Midas ran down the stairs, each step turned to gold. He ran outside to the rose garden. As he touched the roses, they turned to gold! Midas skipped to the breakfast table and waited for Marygold. She was crying as she came in. "My child, what is the matter?" Midas asked.

Without a word Marygold showed her father a golden rose.

"Beautiful!" exclaimed Midas. "But why should such a lovely rose make you cry?"

"It's not beautiful," Marygold sobbed. "It's ugly, and it has lost its sweet smell. What could have happened to all our roses?"

"Please don't cry," King Midas said. He was too ashamed to admit he had turned the roses to gold. "We'll have breakfast, and you'll feel better."

As Marygold began to eat, Midas poured himself some tea from a sparkling gold teapot. He lifted the tea to his lips. The instant the tea touched him, it turned to gold—hard, cold gold. He tried some toast, and this, too, turned to gold. He tried eggs and then a potato. Each thing turned to gold! How was he going to eat? He tried to cram a potato into his mouth and swallow it quickly. The potato instantly turned to gold. Midas roared in pain!

"Father!" Marygold screamed. "Have you burnt your mouth?" Marygold reached out to comfort her father and was instantly turned to gold!

Midas jumped back in disbelief. What terrible thing had he done? Nothing could be worse than this! He hated the golden touch! He hated his greed! He hung his head in despair.

"Are you pleased with your gift?" a voice asked. Midas looked up to see the stranger and began to sob.

"What's wrong?" asked the man. "I kept my word and gave you the golden touch. Did you not get all the things you desired?"

Midas shook his head and began to wring his

hands. "Gold is not everything. My daughter has been turned to gold. Nothing could be worse!"

"So you have changed your mind?" asked the stranger. "Which is worth more now, King Midas, the golden touch or a crust of bread?"

"A crust of bread is worth more than all the gold in the world," Midas replied.

"A cup of water or the golden touch?" asked the man.

"Water!" Midas cried.

"The golden touch or your Marygold?" the stranger asked at last.

"If only I could have my child back! She is worth more than all the riches in the world!" cried Midas.

"You are indeed a much wiser man," the stranger said. "Do not worry. I will tell you what to do."

"Please, enough!" cried Midas. "What can I do?"

"Go plunge yourself into the river," said the man. "Then fill a pitcher with water and bring it back.

Sprinkle the water on everything you have turned to gold. If you try, you might be able to repair the damage you have done."

Midas ran to the river and jumped in without removing any of his clothes. He filled his pitcher with water and hurried back. He sprinkled handfuls of water on the little golden girl. As the water fell on her, she became herself again. But she was dripping wet!

"Father!" she cried. "What are you doing?"

But Midas did not stop to tell her. Instead he ran around sprinkling water on all the things he had touched. Happily he watched as the roses changed from gold back to white and pink and red.

"Beautiful!" he said. "Simply beautiful!" He gave his daughter a rose and gently kissed her forehead.

From then on King Midas hated the very sight of gold. And he was happier than he had ever been.

Mr. Nobody

I know a funny little man,
As quiet as a mouse,
Who does the mischief that is done
In everybody's house!
There's no one ever sees his face,
And yet we all agree
That every plate we break was cracked
By Mr. Nobody.

It's he who always tears our books,
Who leaves the door ajar.
He pulls the buttons from our shirts
And scatters pins afar.
That squeaking door will always squeak,
For, goodness, don't you see,
We leave the oiling to be done
By Mr. Nobody.

The finger marks upon the door
By none of us are made.
We never leave the blinds unclosed
To let the curtains fade.
The ink we never spill. The boots
That lie around, you see,
Are not our boots. They all belong
To Mr. Nobody.

true
blue
glue
due

color

too   blue   due   true
true   glue   blue   tree
glue   true

A Girl in Space

One Friday afternoon Tam and Pam were playing ball in Pam's yard. Tam threw a fast ball to Pam, but Pam couldn't catch it. The ball went through the fence and landed in the next yard.

"I don't think I'll ever be any good at baseball," said Pam.

Tam said, "Well, you don't expect to be a baseball player when you grow up, do you?"

"I don't know what I want to be, Tam," said Pam. "Grandpa thinks I should be a sailor. But I don't think so."

"There's one kind of crew I'd like to join," said Tam, "a crew of astronauts on a spaceship."

"So would I!" said Pam. "I'd like to be in orbit in that blue sky up there right now."

"The sky isn't blue when you're in orbit," said Tam. "It's black."

"How do you know that's true?" asked Pam.

"From reading newspapers and books and watching TV," said Tam. "You can learn a lot that way if you're really interested in something."

For the rest of the afternoon they talked about space travel. Tam knew a good bit about it. First she drew a rocket in the dirt with a stick. Then she told Pam how much some rockets weigh, how tall they are, and how they work.

At last it began to get dark, and Tam said, "It's time for me to go home."

"Stay and have dinner with us," said Pam.

"I wish you could eat at my house instead," said Tam. "Then you could look at my book on space travel. It's due back at the library tomorrow."

Pam asked her father if she could have dinner with Tam's family. But Mr. Sands said, "Pam, we're having beef stew tonight. I know you like it better than almost anything else. You can eat at Tam's house another time."

Pam could tell her father wanted her to stay home, so she said, "Good-by, Tam. I'll see your library book first thing in the morning, if that's all right."

There were very few good programs on TV that night. Pam looked through some magazines for pictures of astronauts and rockets. Her grandmother said she could cut them out of the old magazines. Pam found so many she thought she could fill a whole scrapbook.

Then Pam took a bath and put on her pajamas. She took out three plastic airplanes. She began to play with them in her room. Then she got sheets of paper in different colors and some glue. She made a model of a rocket. She got on her bed and pretended that the rocket was getting ready for lift-off.

At eleven o'clock her dad and grandmother were in the living room when a funny sound came from upstairs. It was Pam counting, "Ten—nine—eight—seven—six—five—four—three—two—one! Blast off!"

"Is Pam still playing up there?" asked Mr. Sands. "Isn't it past her bedtime?"

But Pam wasn't playing. She was in the middle of a dream about space. She was saying, "We're due to fire our rockets now, aren't we, Tam?"

In the dream, Tam was also strapped into a seat. She checked her instruments and said, "Yes, we're due to fire the rockets for the next stage of the flight. We're exactly one hundred miles from Earth."

Pam unfastened her seat belt and got up to look out a window. Suddenly she was floating about the cabin. She had forgotten that people become weightless in space. "Stop me, Tam," she called.

"Who's up there playing with Pam at this time of night?" asked Mr. Sands.

"She's alone," said Pam's grandma. "She must be dreaming and talking in her sleep."

In Pam's space dream, it was now dinner time. The space crew had its meals from tubes filled with food. There was nothing to bite or chew, but Pam's food tasted like beef stew.

As soon as Tam and Pam began to eat, something went wrong with Tam's tube. A drop that looked like gravy floated around near Tam's mouth. At last Tam caught it and ate it. Pam was glad, for she knew it would have been bad to have the gravy splash on the instruments.

Next Pam thought a giant bird was flying past the window of the spaceship. She said to herself, "It's impossible for a bird to be flying around up here." But the bird kept coming back. Then Pam saw that it was another spaceship. Suddenly the color of the strange ship changed from blue to red. Then it blew up. That made Pam's ship explode, too. Pam gasped with fright as she felt herself falling through space. Cold air was blowing across her back.

A second after Pam hit the floor, her father was upstairs. He called, "Mom, you should see this! Pam's pajama top is ripped all the way down the back. And she's upset her night table and her glass of water. That must have been quite a dream!"

Pam didn't know whether she was awake or not. She just kept yelling, "Splashdown! Splashdown!"

guess

guest

guard

guide

guilty

guitar

Helping Hands

There were two quick knocks at the farmhouse door, then two more. A low growl came from the dog in the kitchen. Kerny was old, but he still thought it was his job to guard the Capek family.

"Who could be knocking on our door at five-thirty in the morning?" Sandy Capek asked her husband.

Carl Capek moved quickly. Through the glass he saw a girl about Abby's age holding a small dog. The girl looked frightened.

Mrs. Capek was right beside her husband as he opened the door. "What's wrong?" she asked.

"My father," gasped the girl. "He's hurt!"

"Come into the house," said Mrs. Capek kindly.

"No," said the girl, "there isn't time for that."

"Can you guide me to him?" Mr. Capek asked.

The girl pointed down the road. Mr. Capek took

his keys from his pocket and said, "I'll get the truck. Tell me about your dad while we're driving."

"My name is Sue Flanigan," said the girl. "Dad was taking me to my Aunt Barbara's for a visit. Last night our car broke down, and Dad left Whiskers with me while he went for help. He didn't come back all night. I tried to make the time go faster by strumming my guitar. As soon as it got light, I started to look for Dad. Whiskers found him lying beside the road. Dad's in terrible pain. He thinks his leg is broken."

When they got to the place where Sue had left her father, they found nothing. Sue's father was gone! All they found were some marks in the dirt.

"I can't let Sue start guessing what might have happened," Mr. Capek said to himself.

"Where can he have gone?" cried Sue. "He couldn't even walk! He was in terrible pain!"

"Well, my guess is he dragged himself along the road. He probably got thirsty. Maybe he dragged himself over to the stream for a drink. Let's look over there," said Mr. Capek.

"Oh, I feel so guilty," said Sue. "I never should have left him!"

"You had no choice," said Mr. Capek. "Come on, now. There's a little stream just to the south. I'll bet it will guide us right to your dad."

As they started toward the stream, Mr. Capek stopped. "Tracks," he thought. "And if my guess is right, it's a mountain lion." He set his foot down right in the middle of the big paw print so Sue would not see it.

"Let's head this way," he said to Sue. But his mind was whirling. A mountain lion wouldn't attack unless it was frightened. But Sue's dad might not know how timid these cats are. He might try to strike the cat. Maybe the lion had cubs to guard. "I must stop this guessing. I've just got to find her dad," he thought.

"Sue, why don't you go back to the house and let me do the looking? Sandy will be worried. You can be her guest until I get back," Mr. Capek said. "It's not far to the house."

Just then someone yelled. "Sue! I'm over here!" Sue ran toward the voice and found her father.

"Oh, Dad!" she cried. "I was so worried! I thought something awful had happened! Why did you come over here? How did you get here?"

"Now just slow down. Let me tell you. Not long after you left, I heard a growl. I looked up at that ridge and saw a big mountain lion. Was I ever scared!" said Sue's father. "Then two little cubs came running up behind her. Well, I thought, if she's guarding her little cubs, I'll just move on. I couldn't stand up, so I dragged myself over here to hide. I am so glad to see you!"

"We'll get you to the hospital," said Mr. Capek. "Your daughter can be our guest until you're well."

"How can I ever thank you?" said Sue's dad.

"Just get better," said Mr. Capek. "That will be thanks enough."

Mountain Lions

Mountain lions are large wild animals of the cat family. Today a small number of mountain lions live in Canada and the United States. Many more live in Mexico and South America. Fully grown mountain lions may be five feet long or more, not including the tail. They may weigh as much as two hundred twenty pounds.

Mountain lions usually hunt for food at night. They feed mainly on old or sick deer. They may kill elk or even skunks. But they seldom attack farm animals or pets. They act very timid toward people. Some people even believe mountain lions are playful and like to make friends. It is quite unlikely that a mountain lion would attack a person.

Photo by Tom McHugh/Photo Researchers, Inc.

action
location
conversation
imagination
suggestion
pollution
imitation
combination
attention

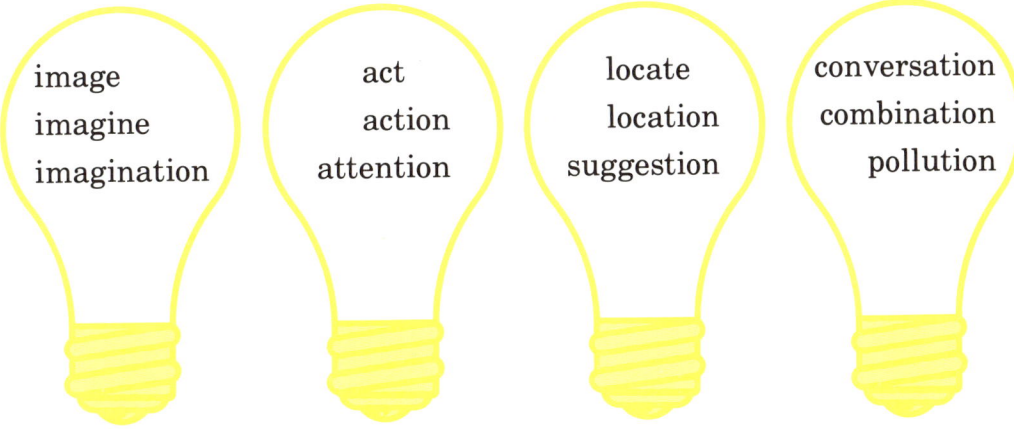

image   act   locate   conversation
imagine   action   location   combination
imagination attention suggestion pollution

Good Ideas

The people of Riverside were planning a contest. The most beautiful block in the city would be chosen. The mayor had heard the idea in a conversation with a man from Grove City.

Mrs. Benton had read about the clean-up drive in Grove City. She was interested since the Bentons had once lived there. But now Riverside was to have a contest, too. She began to worry.

"Do you think the people on our block will pitch in?" she asked her neighbor.

"I think so, if we don't plan to do expensive things," said Ms. Knox.

"What are they talking about?" Jim asked Joan. Joan Knox had come to the Bentons' with her mother.

Joan had heard the same conversation before. She told Jim, "My mom is on the Action Team for this block. So are Mr. Smith and Miss Beck. I guess there are lots of teams in other locations."

"What do they do?" asked Kim.

"They talk to the people on the block about making the street look better," said Joan. "My mother and some others want to plant flowers."

That evening Mrs. Benton, Jim, and Kim told Mr. Benton about Ms. Knox's visit. "We're supposed to grow flowers, Dad," said Jim.

"Is that true? Or is it just Jim's imagination?" Mark asked Sally.

"It was just a suggestion," said Mrs. Benton.

"Well," said Mr. Benton, "I don't like imitation. The people of Grove City planted flowers. We ought to do something different."

"It doesn't have to be the same," said his wife. "Grove City planted their flowers in window boxes. We can plant ours beside the streets."

Neighbors in each block made their plans. One street would have marigolds along the edge of the sidewalks. Some people had felt that pollution from cars might kill the flowers. But they were outvoted, and the seeds were planted.

A number of people on the Bentons' street voted to paint the shutters on their houses. The most popular suggestion was for red shutters. But two houses were yellow, and three others were green. "The combination of red shutters with those colors is not good," the neighbors said. So a different plan was approved.

The sidewalks were painted to look like a garden. People painted flowers in lots of shapes, sizes, and colors. The shutters of the houses had flowers painted on them, too. Above the street hung a giant banner that read "Welcome to the Garden Street garden!"

The mayor did not award first prize to Garden Street. But in his speech he said, "This is what I call using your imagination. Your flowers will not even need attention if you are away on vacation. Changing Garden Street into a garden was a great idea!"

Illustration by Carol Newsom

The Secret
Gladys Baker Bond

"Hey, what's-your-name, how many out-of-state cars did you count?"

Nino heard the words, but he didn't know they were being shouted at him.

Billy put his hands on his hips and looked at Nino. All the other boys who were playing the game looked at Nino, too.

"How many cars?" Billy repeated.

Nino looked at the ground. Then he looked at the high blue sky. He looked at the lines of cars on the street. The cars purred like kittens as they passed. BUT THEY ALL LOOKED ALIKE to Nino. What was an out-of-state car?

How could Nino play the counting game when he didn't even know the rules?

"No cars!" Nino said. He blinked so he wouldn't have to cry in front of Billy.

Adapted from *Little Stories* by Gladys Baker Bond, copyright 1964, with permission of the Anti-Defamation League of B'nai Brith, New York, New York.

Billy laughed and ran back to the head of the line. "What's-his-name can't count out-of-state cars!"

Because Billy laughed, all the other boys laughed, too. Nino curled his fingers in his pockets. That helped him to hold back his tears, but it didn't help him to count out-of-state cars!

"What's your name? somebody asked.

"My—name—is—Nino," Nino said very carefully.

"Where did you come from?" Joe Jeff seemed to sing the words.

"From Italy," Nino said.

"Italy?" Joe Jeff's eyes sparkled. "Wow! You had to cross an ocean!"

What Joe Jeff said made Nino feel better. His fingers began to uncurl in his pockets. Shyly he smiled at Joe Jeff.

"I—I—don't—have—any—out—of—state—cars!" Nino finally admitted.

"Oh, what does that matter? You've crossed an ocean! Anybody can count cars!"

"I can't," Nino admitted. He hung his head. More than anything, Nino wanted a friend in this new land. But would Joe Jeff want a friend who couldn't even play games?

Joe Jeff moved closer to Nino and held out his hand. It felt warm and friendly.

"I'll tell you a secret," Joe Jeff whispered in Nino's ear. "Just look at the license plates!"

"License?" Nino looked at the next car to pass. It was long and shiny, but what was a license?

"See those metal things with numbers and letters on them?" Joe Jeff said.

Nino looked so hard he felt dizzy. The cars zipped by so fast he couldn't read the numbers and the strange letters. Every license was a different color.

"But—there are—so very many!" Nino said and curled his fingers again.

"There's more to the secret," Joe Jeff said as his feet bounced along the sidewalk. "Every state has a different color."

"I can't do it!" Nino said. "So many states—so many colors!"

"Now, look," Joe Jeff said when a red truck passed. "See that black and white license? That belongs to OUR state. If it isn't our state, it's an out-of-state car. Now, you can learn one license, can't you?"

"You like these out-of-state cars?" Nino asked Joe Jeff.

"Oh, sure! They've been some place we haven't been. And maybe the people in those cars have done something we haven't done!"

Now Nino's fingers didn't feel like curling into fists in his pockets. There were so many things to learn in this new land. ONE at a time, he would learn them. It was easy with a friend to share the SECRETS!

Suddenly Nino's feet felt like dancing. Far down

the block he saw a green compact, and it DIDN'T have a black and white license.

"Out-of-state car!" Nino shouted, first and loudest.

Billy looked at Nino. Joe Jeff looked at Nino. So did all the other boys, but this time Nino liked it. They were all smiling.

Reading a Work Schedule

Jon just got a part-time job. He will have several duties to perform. Can you help Jon read his new work schedule?

Time	Monday	Wednesday	Saturday
8:30 to 12:30			Clean up County Stadium.
4:00 to 5:30	Clean up yard at Fifteenth and Main Streets.	Unload office and building supplies at 834 Maple Canyon Drive.	Same as Monday.
6:00 to 7:30	Clean up yard at 11911 East Center Avenue.		Unload lumber at 756 West Mound Street.

TO THE TEACHER

The MERRILL LINGUISTIC READING PROGRAM consists of eight Readers developed on linguistic principles applicable to the teaching of reading. The rationale of the program and detailed teaching procedures are described in the Teacher's Edition of each Reader.

All words introduced in this Reader are listed on the following pages under the headings "Words in Pattern," "Sight Words," and "Applications of Patterning."

Words listed as "Words in Pattern" represent additional minor sets of spelling patterns.

Words listed as "Sight Words" are high-frequency words introduced to provide normal sentence patterns in the stories.

Words listed as "Applications of Patterning" include new words based on patterns and sight words previously introduced, combinations of words (compound words), additional tense forms, plurals, possessives, and contractions.

WORD LISTS FOR TEACHER REFERENCE

Pages	Words in Pattern	Sight Words	Pages	Words in Pattern	Sight Words
Unit 1 5-10	live give forgive olive		Unit 6 45-54 cont.	month won wonder	
Unit 2 11-20	love glove shove cover done none once	warm	Unit 7 55-62	find kind mind wind wild mild child	nothing
Unit 3 21-26	head dead read ready bread thread instead already	aquarium	Unit 8 63-68	put push pull full post most almost	young
Unit 4 27-38	sweat sweater breath leather weather heavy	floor buy special	Unit 9 69-76	food mood moon spoon	four
Unit 5 39-44	wear bear tear pear	busy business high	Unit 10 77-82	toot boot root groove roof proof	again
Unit 6 45-54	earth earn learn early	two	Unit 11 83-90	owl howl fowl prowl growl	calf half

Pages	Words in Pattern	Sight Words
Unit 12 91-96	chief thief grief belief relief believe relieve	
Unit 13 97-104	oil boil soil spoil broil join joint point appoint noise	idea
Unit 14 105-112	toy employ annoy destroy great break steak	eye
Unit 15 113-118	ought fought brought thought	cough

Pages	Words in Pattern	Sight Words
Unit 15 113-118 cont.	caught taught naughty daughter	
Unit 16 119-128	rough tough enough word worry worse worst worth	beautiful
Unit 17 129-134	true blue glue due	color
Unit 18 135-140	guess guest guard guide guilty guitar	
Unit 19 141-151	action location conversation imagination suggestion pollution imitation combination attention	

Applications of Patterning
(The underlined numbers are page numbers.)

Unit 1 5-10	Unit 2 11-20 cont.	Unit 2 11-20 cont.	Unit 3 21-26-cont.
ambulance	angry	slaves	snagged
beef	army	soon	snails
cleaned	battle	South	spoken
cleaner	birthday	spite	stale
clearly	catcher's	Springfield	stones
connected	cheer	Tad	sunbath
counter	covered	United	turtle
county	dancing	War	turtles
emergency	dishwasher	Washington	turtle's
ends	disturbed	Willie	underwater
exact	disturbing	worn	untangle
feels	ears		
filling	elected	Unit 3 21-26	
following	Fido		Unit 4 27-38
heater	friends	Abby	
listed	generals	afternoon	accept
lived	gloves	answer	amazing
managed	harder	certainly	battery
moving	jeans	clever	bending
new	jogged	cloudy	blocking
odds	jogging	crawl	brace
olives	Lincoln	dirty	brothers
page	Lincolns	Friday	buttons
phone	Lincoln's	harden	buying
police	living	heads	buzzed
salad	loves	huddle	champion
scrub	men's	Jen	chance
sheets	North	Jennifer	chilly
sheriff	Northern	Jenny	clothes
shiver	office	lockers	coach
spare	ours	moved	college
sweeper	oven	November	compete
telephone	partly	overfeed	concerned
unloading	pitcher's	possible	credit
unpacked	pony	prove	customers
upstairs	President	questions	darting
without	President's	remove	dashing
	promise	return	delivered
Unit 2 11-20	restless	scarf	disease
	restlessly	scratched	doctors
Abe	Roll	shady	dribbling
above	salads	slugs	escalator
Abraham	shoved	smelling	everybody
	since		

Applications of Patterning
(The underlined numbers are page numbers.)

Unit 4 27-38 cont.	Unit 4 27-38 cont.	Unit 5 39-44 cont.	Unit 6 45-54
examined	scholarship	blinked	allowed
except	seventeenth	blur	anywhere
fabric	shifts	butterflies	athlete
favorite	sickly	Case	basketballs
fever	sisters	Casey	Celtics
finally	sixty	Casey's	corners
fussed	Skeeter	cheerful	denim
girls'	sleet	corridor	divided
given	speed	Dallas	driveways
graceful	spunky	daydreaming	earned
grown	stalled	detector	eighteen
hopeful	stricken	dream	exercise
impressed	struggled	faded	Fame
improvement	supply	flew	few
invited	survived	formed	final
Italy	sweaters	gone	folded
Jane's	Temple	higher	gym
knitting	Tennessee	highest	gyms
Lane's	terrible	highways	hanger
limp	tested	jerked	helps
linings	thirteen	Kay	indoor
loved	thousand	kisses	James
massage	Tigerbelle	lifting	knees
massaged	Tigerbelles	mist	Knicks
massaging	treatments	mounds	Lakers
medals	trimming	mountains	learned
nickname	unlucky	mouth	loudly
ninety	University	nervous	Massachusetts
noses	urged	quietly	mended
Olympic	weighed	realized	millions
Olympics	Wilma	reassure	moments
overcome	Wilma's	runway	Naismith
parents	women's	scolded	Naismith's
poked	yarn	seat	only
polio	yesterday's	shall	opening
poor		she'd	patches
practiced	Unit 5 39-44	soft	Pistons
present		stared	practice
prodded		surely	prepared
puffs	airplanes	thrilling	preparing
Rome	arrived	throwing	prize
Rudolph	assured	tingly	published
salesclerk	attendant	waving	rule
scarlet	below	whipped	rules

Applications of Patterning
(The underlined numbers are page numbers.)

Unit 6 45-54 cont.	Unit 7 55-62 cont.	Unit 8 63-68 cont.	Unit 9 69-76 cont.
score	person's	magazines	cow
scoring	reel	makeup	creatures
soccer	reels	meats	cud
sports	replace	medicine	cuds
teams	seas	medicines	Debby
tears	seashore	mistakes	digest
tore	shark	newspapers	drifts
walking	sinkers	ordered	ear
wearing	smelts	pose	else
wondered	sunrise	posts	examine
wonderful	tangle	prescription	extended
YMCA	tangled	prescriptions	fighters
zero	thirty	pulls	firehouse
	thrown	puts	flick
Unit 7 55-62	traps	puzzles	forehead
	turns	rainstorm	friend
adult	weights	rainy	frightened
bait	whip	reads	Ginny
baited	winds	scrubbing	Ginny's
batting		shaving	giraffe's
bird's	Unit 8 63-68	shoppers	grateful
boats		shovels	grew
canned	ale	sidewalk	hairs
captain	blows	snow	height
cast	bottles	sprays	herd
certain	bull	sweeps	herds
daylight	capsules	toothpaste	Jenson
falls	counters	waits	Jenson's
fights	counts	walks	mooing
finding	customer	works	movement
fishhooks	deliver		nibble
hooked	door	Unit 9 69-76	noon
kinds	doorbell		operate
law	drug		owner
lines	druggist	Africa	peaceful
managing	druggists	alert	peeks
markets	drugs	answered	plains
Martin	drugstore	awkward	puzzled
mile	errands	banner	quiet
minds	Farr	behind	shadows
nibbles	Farr's	bulls	silently
outdoors	goods	chew	skyline
party	helper	chewed	slender
penny	holding	chewing	smallest

Applications of Patterning
(The underlined numbers are page numbers.)

Unit 9 69-76 cont.	Unit 10 77-82 cont.	Unit 11 83-90 cont.	Unit 12 91-96 cont.
something's	purse	lives	hearing
spoonful	raining	located	Jeff
stomach	rainwater	Mead	leaving
stomachs	rattles	Minna	platform
stores	recorders	minute	plunge
straddle	records	museum	relieved
studying	singing	neighing	roping
swallows	slapping	newborn	rustlers
tense	stamping	nightshirt	search
they'd	striking	often	stamped
twitch	sung	Papa	stampede
unchewed	Thursday	parents'	stealing
upward	trumpet	Perez	thieves
veterinarian	turntable	poem	trace
wrinkled	wringing	proves	trample
yellow	X-rays	prowling	western
		remind	
Unit 10 77-82	Unit 11 83-90	rooster	Unit 13 97-104
		Rosa	
against	aha	shows	Anthony
bodies	awake	slowed	appetite
boots	barn	surround	appointed
closet	Bedford	Tomas	batch
concerts	cackle	tomorrow	Bay
emptying	Carlos	trailer	bowl
example	cone	Vince	broiled
flutes	delighted	wakened	broiling
forgetting	depended	Wednesday	carrots
French	Dobbs	wobbly	channel
Gretel	eel		disappointed
Hansel	electric	Unit 12 91-96	Eddy
hollow	farmhand		fold
horn	frisky		fruit
instrument	Hays	answers	Hilda
instruments	hitching	branding	homemade
jaw	hoot	campfires	joints
kettle	Kathy's	cliff	juice
marimba	Lane	cowhand	Kenny
musical	lantern	cowhands	measure
own	Liberty	cowpuncher's	measuring
practicing	licking	death	mixture
puddle	line's	exactly	mushrooms
pulled	listening	follow	odd

158

Applications of Patterning
(The underlined numbers are page numbers.)

Unit 13 97-104 cont.	Unit 14 105-112 cont.	Unit 15 113-118 cont.	Unit 16 119-128 cont.
orange	grumbled	football	heaps
peel	hi	gardening	hurried
pepper	housetop	headed	imagined
pitchers	laden	interrupted	instant
pitches	larger	mistake	instantly
platters	lawn	movies	lifetime
pointed	lie	news	Marygold
Polly	Lin	newspaper	Midas
pour	lovely	pennies	mischief
pretzel	membership	radio	mouse
putting	pouted	revolving	nobody
raincoats	renew	saving	oiling
rained	sign	sniffle	palace
salt	silence	taxi	potato
sections	snowflakes	vase	poured
shirts	softly	vases	ray
slice	sold		removing
slices	sorry		repair
Smith	stares	Unit 16 119-128	replied
spoiled	Sue		riches
spread	toys	admit	roared
stalk	twelve	afar	scatters
stir	whispered	ajar	simply
strawberries	widened	amount	skipped
tablespoon	winked	blinds	sob
thawed		bother	sobbed
thawing	Unit 15 113-118	breakfast	sparkled
throw		burnt	sparkling
towels	arts	coins	sprinkle
vinegar	backfired	comfort	sprinkled
wedges	bought	cram	sprinkling
yogurt	broth	curtains	squeak
	cement	desired	squeaking
Unit 14 105-112	chunks	despair	sunbeam
	coin	disbelief	swallow
blade	contents	everybody's	teapot
bushes	counted	exclaimed	toast
comic	crashed	finger	touch
complaining	crazy	gazed	touched
confused	decided	granted	touching
enjoys	doors	greed	treasure
eyes	editor	handfuls	unclosed
gather	faked	handsome	voice
		hated	watched

159

Applications of Patterning
(The underlined numbers are page numbers.)

Unit 16 119-128 cont.	Unit 18 135-140	Unit 18 135-140 cont.	Unit 19 141-151 cont.
wealthy	Abby's	toward	Joan
wiser	America	unlikely	Joe
wring	attack	usually	Jon
	awful	whirling	Knox
	Barbara's	Whiskers	Knox's
Unit 17 129-134	Canada	worried	license
	Capek		locate
	choice		locations
astronauts	elk		loudest
bedtime	Flanigan	Unit 19 141-151	marigolds
blew	foot		Mound
colors	fully		Nino
counting	guarding	admitted	Nino's
crew	guessing	anybody	ocean
dreaming	including	approved	outvoted
drew	keys	Avenue	pockets
explode	kindly	award	popular
fence	knocking	Beck	purred
gravy	knocks	Billy	repeated
impossible	lion	Canyon	schedule
pajama	lions	changing	secret
pajamas	lying	chosen	shapes
pictures	mainly	compact	shutters
programs	Mexico	curled	shyly
scrapbook	mountain	curling	sidewalks
spaceship	paw	duties	somebody
splash	playful	expensive	speech
splashdown	seldom	Fifteenth	stadium
stew	strumming	friendly	supplies
strapped	Sue's	hey	tears
threw	thirsty	hips	uncurl
unfastened	timid	ideas	unload
watching		imagine	voted
weightless		Jeff's	words

160